DATE			

604

BAKER & TAYLOR

LEWIS AND CLARK

Other titles in *Historical American Biographies*

Annie Oakley
Legendary Sharpshooter
ISBN 0-7660-1012-0

John Wesley Powell
Explorer of the Grand Canyon
ISBN 0-89490-783-2

Benjamin Franklin
Founding Father and Inventor
ISBN 0-89490-784-0

Lewis and Clark
Explorers of the Northwest
ISBN 0-7660-1016-3

Buffalo Bill Cody
Western Legend
ISBN 0-7660-1015-5

Martha Washington
First Lady
ISBN 0-7660-1017-1

Clara Barton
Civil War Nurse
ISBN 0-89490-778-6

Paul Revere
Rider for the Revolution
ISBN 0-89490-779-4

Jeb Stuart
Confederate Cavalry General
ISBN 0-7660-1013-9

Robert E. Lee
Southern Hero of the Civil War
ISBN 0-89490-782-4

Jefferson Davis
President of the Confederacy
ISBN 0-7660-1064-3

Stonewall Jackson
Confederate General
ISBN 0-89490-781-6

Jesse James
Legendary Outlaw
ISBN 0-7660-1055-4

Susan B. Anthony
Voice for Women's Voting Rights
ISBN 0-89490-780-8

Thomas Alva Edison
Inventor
ISBN 0-7660-1014-7

Historical American Biographies

LEWIS AND CLARK

Explorers of the Northwest

ANTHONY QUINN LIB. 604
3965 E. CESAR CHAVEZ AVE.
LOS ANGELES, CA 90063
(323) 264-7715

Tom Streissguth

Enslow Publishers, Inc.

40 Industrial Road	PO Box 38
Box 398	Aldershot
Berkeley Heights, NJ 07922	Hants GU12 6BP
USA	UK

http://www.enslow.com

Copyright © 1998 by Tom Streissguth

Library of Congress Cataloging-in-Publication Data

Streissguth, Thomas, 1958–
    Lewis and Clark : explorers of the Northwest / Tom Streissguth.
       p. cm. — (Historical American biographies)
    Includes bibliographical references (p.) and index.
    Summary: Traces the lives, careers, and achievements of the two men
who, under instructions from President Jefferson, explored the American
Northwest and the lands of the Louisiana Purchase.
    ISBN 0-7660-1016-3
    1. Lewis, Meriwether, 1774–1809—Juvenile literature. 2. Clark,
William, 1770–1838—Juvenile literature. 3. Explorers—West (U.S.)—
Biography—Juvenile literature. 4. Lewis and Clark Expedition
(1804–1806)—Juvenile literature. 5. West (U.S.)—Discovery and
exploration—Juvenile literature. [1. Lewis, Meriwether, 1774–1809.
2. Clark, William, 1770–1838. 3. Explorers. 4. Lewis and Clark
Expedition (1804–1806) 5. West (U.S.)—Discovery and exploration.]
I. Title. II. Series.
F592.7.S76 1998
917.804'2—dc21   97-18044
                                    CIP
                                     AC

Printed in the United States of America

10 9 8 7 6 5 4 3 2

CONTENTS

1

AT MARIAS RIVER

In the early evening of June 2, 1805, the thirty-three members of the Lewis and Clark expedition began preparing their campsite. They had reached a level bank along the southern shore of the Missouri—the river they had been exploring for more than a year. While the men built shelters and sparked their campfires, Meriwether Lewis and William Clark looked across the river, taking in a troubling sight.

On the northern, right-hand side, the two captains could see a wide stream joining the river. This stream came from the west, and like the Missouri, its waters were muddy and slow. A left-hand fork veered off to the south, but its water was clear. "An

This map shows the forks in the Missouri River, where Lewis and Clark had to determine which route they should take toward the Pacific Ocean.

interesting question was now to be determined," Lewis wrote in his journal that night, "which of these rivers was the Missouri."[1]

A few months before reaching this spot, Lewis and Clark had questioned the people of the Hidatsa tribe about the upper Missouri. The Hidatsa had described the river and its tributaries—the smaller waterways that emptied into the Missouri along its winding course. They had traced a map in the ground that showed how the river turned among steep bluffs and open plains. But they had not described this fork in the river. Instead of another tributary, Lewis and Clark were expecting to reach a waterfall.[2] According to the Hidatsa, somewhere near this campsite a great cascade of water tumbled over high cliffs, sending clouds of mist into the air. To follow the Missouri, the captains would have to portage (travel by land between two waterways) around the falls. Farther upriver, the Missouri would divide into three forks. Here the explorers would have to follow the western fork to reach the trail that led across the Rocky Mountains.

Was the right-hand river they now saw the Missouri, which it resembled? Or did the Missouri continue south, to the left? On June 4, Lewis took a small party along the right-hand stream, while Clark set out along the southern fork. After the captains returned to the camp, they announced their decision: The northern stream was a tributary. It ran for a long distance through the plains, picking up the sediment that muddied its waters. The southern branch was the real Missouri. It came a shorter distance from its source, so its waters were clearer. This fork would lead them to the great waterfall.

Lewis and Clark were certain of it.[3] Lewis even gave the right-hand stream a name: Marias River,

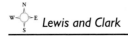
Lewis and Clark

The Corps of Discovery was attempting to reach the Great Falls of the Missouri River when they were stumped by a fork in the river.

after his cousin Maria Wood. But the other members of the expedition disagreed. From camp, the Marias River seemed to lead directly to the mountains, and it must be the true Missouri. If the captains were wrong, they would waste valuable time. If they were late reaching the mountains, the early winter and the high, snowbound trails would block their passage to the Pacific Ocean. The expedition would have to turn back downriver, and the mission would fail.

In the summer and fall of 1803, Lewis and Clark had carefully selected these men for their courage

and stamina. All of them—sergeants, privates, and guides—could handle themselves in the wilderness. Over the past months, they had developed another important trait: loyalty to the two captains. Lewis and Clark had seen them safely through terrible storms, dangerous river currents, a hostile encounter with the Sioux, and running fights with ferocious brown bears. Now the soldiers and guides would follow. On the evening of June 9, Lewis wrote in his journal: "all [of the members of the expedition] . . . except Capt. C being still firm in the belief that the N. Fork was the Missouri and that which we ought to take; [but] they said very cheerfully that they were ready to follow us any wher we thought proper to direct."[4]

To make sure, the captains would split the

Meriwether Lewis, pictured here wearing a suit of animal hides, followed the course of the left-hand river to find the great waterfall.

party. On Tuesday, June 11, Lewis picked four men and set out overland, to solve the mystery as soon as possible. He followed the general course of the left-hand river and found that it ran south and then to the southwest. Clark continued up the river with the rest of the expedition and the boats. Two days later, Lewis heard a steady rumble coming from behind great white clouds of vapor. He recognized this sound as the roar of an immense waterfall.

In a few hours, Lewis would discover the Great Falls of the Missouri River. In a few weeks, the Lewis and Clark expedition would reach the Rocky Mountains.

2

THE LEWISES
OF LOCUST
HILL

The Lewis family had been settled in the British colonies of America since 1635.[1] In that year, a Welsh officer named Robert Lewis landed in the New World. Over the years, Robert Lewis and his descendants had bought and were granted thousands of acres of wilderness. They cleared and planted the land, selling their Virginia tobacco to markets in the colonies and in the British Isles. Like many other planters, they also speculated in land, counting on the arrival of new settlers to drive up prices for their property. Robert Lewis's son, also named Robert, left large plantations to each of his nine children. One of these, Locust Hill, an estate of nearly two thousand acres in Albemarle County in central Virginia, was passed to his son William Lewis.

In 1769, William Lewis married his cousin Lucy Meriwether, who also belonged to a family of Virginia landowners. Their first child was a daughter named Jane. On August 18, 1774, Meriwether Lewis was born. Three years later, William and Lucy Lewis had another son, Reuben.

In the summer of 1775, when Meriwether Lewis was still an infant, Virginia and the other British colonies were preparing to fight for independence. Like most Albemarle County planters, William Lewis supported this fight, seeing it as the best way to end the taxes, regulations, and restrictions imposed by the British governor of Virginia. Lewis volunteered to serve in a local militia, the Albemarle County Minutemen. Along with his unit, William Lewis later joined the Continental Army, the regular army of the rebellious colonies.

The Squire of Locust Hill

The British were not the only danger William Lewis and other colonial officers faced. In November 1779, while returning to his unit after a leave, Lewis crossed the swollen Rivanna River. He slipped from his horse and fell into the icy water. Two days later, he died of pneumonia. Nicholas Lewis, William's brother, became the legal guardian of the three

Lewis children. As the oldest son in the family, Meriwether Lewis inherited the buildings, land, and slaves of Locust Hill.

In the spring of 1780, Lucy Meriwether married her second husband, John Marks, who had also served in the Continental Army. After the Americans won the Revolutionary War in 1783, Marks brought his wife and stepchildren south to the Broad River valley of northern Georgia. British raids had left many Virginia farms and fields in ruins, and planters were moving south to clear land in a region untouched by the war. Meriwether Lewis would spend several years in Georgia, while his uncle Nicholas managed the estate at Locust Hill.

There were no schools to attend in Georgia, and very few tutors available for private lessons. Instead of instruction in Latin, mathematics, geography, and other traditional subjects, Meriwether Lewis studied hunting, trapping, and natural science in the trackless forests of the Broad River region. He spent much of his time rambling in the woods, forging his own paths, hunting for food, and learning how to survive in the wilderness. He studied plants and animals, learning a great deal from his mother, who was an expert in collecting and using wild herbs. Meriwether also learned how to handle himself in dangerous situations. He once coolly faced down a charging bull in the forest, and according to one familiar story, he once saved the Broad River settlers by dousing a fire during an Indian raid.

But Meriwether needed formal schooling, as well as instruction in the management of Locust Hill. When he turned thirteen, his family sent him back to Albemarle County to study. From a Virginia parson, Matthew Maury, he learned Latin, history, natural science, and mathematics. He also studied with the Reverend James Waddell and Dr. Charles Everitt, a physician who proved to be an impatient and temperamental master.

In the summer of 1791, when he was just turning seventeen, Meriwether Lewis helped his mother, who had been widowed for a second time, return to Locust Hill. He brought a carriage from Virginia to Georgia and then transported household goods, livestock, slaves, and family—his mother, brother, sister, half brother, and half sister—back to Albemarle County along hundreds of miles of narrow, often unmarked trails. Lewis liked nothing better than to strike out on such a long journey, blazing trails where necessary and exploring unknown forests and mountains. He was at his best in the wilderness, as his moody temperament made dealing with people in a more civilized setting difficult.

Now seventeen years old, Meriwether Lewis may have had plans for an education at William and Mary, the college at Williamsburg, Virginia, which was attended by many other planters' sons. But his property and his family also demanded attention. The advice of the elders in the family was for Lewis to quit his schooling and move into the house at Locust Hill. Lewis agreed, reluctantly, and took up the familiar life of a Virginia plantation owner. He would direct the planting and harvesting of crops, the care of a livestock herd, and the supervision of the two dozen slaves who worked on the estate.

The Whiskey Rebellion

Nicholas Lewis had spent years preparing his nephew for this work, but the management of Locust Hill was of little interest to Meriwether Lewis.[2] He was restless, ambitious, and, like his father had been, prone to fits of depression. Missing his adventures in the wilderness, he began searching for an opportunity to break free of his secure and settled life. In 1792, when he was eighteen, he volunteered for a western expedition being planned by Secretary of State Thomas Jefferson. Jefferson had been a friend of William Lewis and was acquainted with Lewis's hardy, self-confident son. Jefferson, however, turned down Meriwether Lewis, believing him too young to lead such a dangerous mission.

Lewis saw another chance for adventure two years later, when a rebellion broke out in western

Pennsylvania and Ohio. Thousands of farmers and settlers on the western frontier were taking up arms against a new tax on whiskey. Alexander Hamilton, secretary of the treasury in President George Washington's administration, planned to levy the tax to raise money for the federal government. Hamilton and Washington also believed the whiskey tax would help the government bring the disorganized frontier territories under greater control.

The whiskey rebels did not see things the same way as Hamilton. On the western frontier, whiskey was a vital product, one that many pioneers depended on to make their living. Currency was scarce, and the settlers often had to use whiskey instead of money when they bought and sold their goods. Now the government proposed to control and tax it, even though the frontier territories enjoyed no representation in the United States Congress.

In the 1770s, the American colonists had also protested taxation without representation, and had fought for their freedom under George Washington. As president, however, Washington saw the Whiskey Rebellion as a direct threat to his country's unity.[3] Determined to put down the revolt, Washington ordered Virginia and other states to raise militias— temporary units that would beef up the small United States Army. Meriwether Lewis and thousands of other young men, eager to emulate the heroic exploits of their fathers in the Revolutionary War, immediately volunteered.

Joining the Virginia militia as a private, Lewis marched with his unit as far as Pittsburgh. In the meantime, however, the show of force by George Washington had intimidated the leaders of the rebellion. In October 1794, they fled west to avoid a fight, and the Whiskey Rebellion ended.

The members of the Virginia militia prepared to march home. But Meriwether Lewis found that he greatly enjoyed the soldier's life.[4] Marching, camping, and the companionship of his fellow soldiers suited him well, and he decided to remain in Pennsylvania with his unit. In the fall of 1794, he earned a promotion to the rank of ensign (the lowest rank of commissioned officer). In May 1795, he transferred to the regular United States Army, where he was assigned to the Second Legion and the command of General "Mad" Anthony Wayne at Fort Greenville, Ohio.

On the Frontier

Meriwether Lewis proved to be a reliable and intelligent officer. General Wayne gave him responsibility for carrying payroll and dispatches through the Ohio wilderness, where Lewis rode thousands of miles over rough trails and through untamed forest. Here Lewis found the isolation and adventure he had

Mad Anthony's Army
In the early 1790s, the United States Army was poorly paid, poorly equipped, and understaffed. The total number of enlisted men and officers was about two thousand. Privates earned only three dollars a month. To fill the gaps in times of need, the government had to raise state militias—companies of amateur soldiers recruited from the nation's townspeople and farmers, and led by their own commanders.

To remedy the situation, the government formed a new, professional army in 1794. "Mad" Anthony Wayne, a veteran commander of the Revolutionary War, was put in charge. Wayne drilled his enlisted men and officers every day. They learned to maneuver together, to build fortifications, and to use their weapons by firing live rounds. Wayne punished disobedience with flogging and sometimes with execution.

always enjoyed. Although he never took part in combat, he had many close calls with starvation and sickness while tramping through the northwestern forests.

Lewis also found adventure in camp. A serious confrontation took place in September 1795, when Lewis barged into an officer's house while drunk. The two men argued. Later, Lewis challenged the officer to a duel. For this, Lewis was brought before a court-martial for violating regulations against using "provocative speech."[5] Although he was found not guilty, Lewis was soon transferred to an infantry unit known as the Chosen Rifle Company.

Despite this brush with military justice, the army rewarded Lewis with greater responsibilities and a promotion. In 1797, Lewis took command of an infantry company at Fort Pickering, on the Mississippi River. When the fort's commander died, Lewis was promoted to commander of the outpost. Later he returned to Ohio, where he continued to serve as a dispatch rider. The army promoted him to lieutenant in March 1799. In December of the next year, he became a captain, with responsibility as a regimental paymaster. In his new post, Lewis handled pay for units stationed all over the frontier. He was also responsible for tracking down soldiers who had deserted the army.

In early March 1801, Lewis received a letter from Thomas Jefferson, who had just taken office as the third president of the United States. Jefferson had appointments to make and much work to carry out. He needed a personal secretary to join him in the President's House (it would not officially be called the White House until 1901). As Jefferson explained to Lewis, "Your knolege of the Western country . . . has rendered it desireable . . . that you should be engaged in that office."[6] As the letter hinted, the president wanted Lewis involved in the planning of a new western exploration.

Meriwether Lewis's experiences with the army on the northwestern frontier would help prepare him to become the co-commander of the Corps of Discovery.

Lewis would have to leave the frontier and the active service he loved. He would not earn much—about the same as his army pay—but he would keep his rank as captain. He would also take part in important decisions at the president's side. "The office is more in the nature of that of an Aid de camp, than a mere Secretary," Jefferson wrote.[7] Other men had asked for the post, but Lewis was the president's first choice. With enthusiasm, the captain accepted.[8] Later in March, he put his army affairs in order and set out with his packhorses and baggage for Washington, D.C.

3

THE CLARKS
OF CAROLINE
COUNTY

The Revolutionary War brought many Virginia men out of their homes and to the army camps and battlefields. In Caroline County, southeast of Albemarle, five of John Clark's six sons—born over a twenty-year span, starting in 1750—volunteered for service against the British. Only the youngest son, William Clark—born on August 1, 1770— stayed home.

The Clarks were descended from a Scottish immigrant who had settled on the James River in the late seventeenth century. The Clarks planted tobacco and built large estates, which by the laws and customs of the colony they willed to their eldest sons. With each new generation, the plantation families of Virginia grew wealthier from the rise in the value of their land. The Clarks, as well as the Lewises, joined a colonial aristocracy that held much of Virginia's economic and political power.

John Clark, the great-grandson of the first Clark immigrant, moved to a four-hundred-acre plantation at the foot of the Blue Ridge Mountains in Albemarle County. The Clark estate lay quite near the tobacco and cornfields of William Lewis. But the country here was not safe from raiding that occurred during the French and Indian War on the North American frontier. Around 1757, John Clark moved eastward to safer territory in Caroline County. There, he and his wife raised six sons and four daughters.

Twenty years later, the Revolutionary War disrupted the lives of the Clarks and other Virginia planters. Nevertheless, the Clarks were loyal to the cause of independence. One of the Clark sons, George Rogers Clark, led a daring campaign against the British on the northwestern frontier. With a company of volunteers recruited from Kentucky and the Ohio River valley, General Clark captured several British outposts, including an important garrison at the town of Vincennes (in what is now Indiana). Clark's campaign prevented the British from gathering their forces for an attack on the Continental Army from the northwest.

The colonies eventually won the Revolution and established the United States. But after saving the Northwest for the young nation, George Rogers Clark, who was never defeated or even surprised in battle, had to struggle with the many debts he had taken on to pay and supply his troops. The United States government would not honor these debts, because Clark had contracted them without the government's authority. Nor would Virginia help, as the state had given up its claim to the northwestern frontier that Clark had secured. Financially ruined and in poor health, a bitter George Rogers Clark came to depend on the help of his devoted younger brother, William Clark.

Fighting on the Northwestern Frontier

After the end of the Revolutionary War, the Clark family left Caroline County. Inspired by George Rogers Clark's description of fertile and cheap land in the Ohio River valley, John Clark moved west to an estate near the frontier town of Louisville, Kentucky, in 1784. The Clarks built an imposing two-story wooden cabin at their new estate, which they called Mulberry Hill.

Here, William Clark may have spent many hours listening to the stories of his elder brothers, four of whom had survived the Revolutionary War. William developed a strong loyalty to the American government and learned to dislike and distrust the British—emotions that would stay with him for the rest of his life. Eager to prove his own mettle, Clark took the first opportunity he had to enlist, joining an expedition of Kentucky militia in 1789, when he was nineteen. Led by Major John Hardin, the forces swept north into the Wabash River valley, where they fought against American Indian bands that had been raiding in Kentucky.

While William Clark was experiencing his first taste of military life and discipline, the United States government was organizing campaigns against other tribes living north of the Ohio River. Although the British had surrendered the lands south of the Great Lakes, a string of British outposts at Detroit and other strategic points still threatened the United States from the northwest. British officers were recruiting the Shawnee, Delaware, and other Ohio valley tribes to raid American settlements and disrupt American trade in the region. In this way, the British hoped to stop American expansion at the Ohio River and keep control of the northwestern fur trade for British companies.

In March 1791, Clark earned a lieutenant's commission in the regular army. While serving under Lieutenant Colonel James Wilkinson in Ohio, he took

Like Meriwether Lewis, William Clark had military experiences as a young man that prepared him to serve as the co-commander of the Corps of Discovery.

part in two raids on the Wea tribes living along the Wabash River. In 1793, while still under Wilkinson's command, Clark's unit joined the campaign of General Anthony Wayne's Legion. Its mission was to put an end to the troubles on the northwestern frontier and reclaim the country that had been won for the colonies by George Rogers Clark.

The Battle of Fallen Timbers

In the summer of 1794, Wayne marched his troops north from Cincinnati, raising Fort Recovery and Fort Greenville in western Ohio. The Legion then pushed on to the Maumee River, where Wayne ordered his men to raise earthworks—protective barriers made of sod, boulders, tree branches, and any other material at hand. Wayne was determined to lure the nearby Indian tribes into a large, decisive battle that would settle control over the Northwest for good.

On the morning of August 20, Wayne saw his chance. Shawnee, Delaware, and Miami warriors had gathered for an ambush among thousands of tangled trees felled by a recent storm. With William Clark's unit reinforcing the main attack, the early-morning battle quickly turned into a rout. The Shawnee and their allies fell back to a British fort, whose commander refused to open the gates and face a direct attack by the Americans. Abandoned

James Wilkinson—Leader and Traitor

William Clark felt a strong loyalty to his commander, Lieutenant Colonel James Wilkinson. Clark may have appreciated Wilkinson's ability as a Revolutionary War fighter, but his faith in Wilkinson as a patriot was misplaced. Wilkinson was, in fact, a traitor.

After the Revolutionary War, Wilkinson swore allegiance to Spain. For his services, the Spanish paid him two thousand dollars a year. In 1805, Wilkinson was serving as the first military governor of the Louisiana Territory. At the same time, he was plotting with then Vice President Aaron Burr to invade Mexico and establish a new nation on the southwestern frontier of the United States.

When Aaron Burr's plot was discovered, Wilkinson had Burr arrested. He then testified against Burr at Burr's trial for treason. Instead of being prosecuted for his own part in the scheme, Wilkinson was cleared of all charges. He left the United States and lived out his final days in Mexico City, where he died in 1825.[1]

by their British allies, the Ohio valley tribes soon ended their raids on Wayne's army.

The Battle of Fallen Timbers marked the end of the campaign against the American Indians and the British in the Northwest. It allowed the United States to secure territory as far west as the

Mississippi River. In the summer of 1795, General Wayne signed the Treaty of Fort Greenville with representatives of all the tribes in the region. In exchange for treaty goods—blankets, tools, and food—to be distributed to them every year, the tribes surrendered their ancestral lands north of the Ohio River. By the time of the treaty, both William Clark and Meriwether Lewis were serving in Wayne's army. Both may have been present at the treaty negotiations as well as at the signing ceremony.

William Clark had earned the trust of his commanders and of the enlisted men serving under him. Having spent six years in the military, Clark was skilled in supply, fortification, and navigation in the wilderness. He had been assigned to espionage missions and had negotiated with Indian leaders. He had also started a close friendship with Meriwether Lewis. The younger Lewis developed great respect for Clark's ability to control and command the restless frontier soldiers. He also learned that Clark was a skilled navigator and mapmaker.

However, there remained important differences between the two men. Although Lewis thrived in the military, Clark, along with many other young men, saw great opportunities opening before him on the newly opened western frontier. "I have some intentions of resigning and getting into some business in Kentucky or on the Mississippi," Clark wrote his

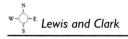

William Clark and Meriwether Lewis were both enlisted in the army under General Anthony Wayne, shown here.

family while still in the army, "As I think there is a great opportunity for an extension of the Mississippi trade in that river could a man form valuable connections in New Orleans."[2] In July 1796, Clark resigned his commission and left the army. While Lewis remained in Ohio, Clark moved back to the family estate at Mulberry Hill.

Family Business

John Clark died in 1799. Fearing that creditors would try to seize land left to George Rogers Clark, he willed much of his estate to his son William. More than seven thousand acres of land, a distillery, and twenty-four slaves passed to William. In exchange for this inheritance, William Clark took on the task of fending off the many lawsuits brought against his elder brother by western traders and merchants.

George Rogers Clark had fallen victim to the whims of bureaucrats and politicians and to sheer bad luck. The state of Virginia had given up its claim to its western county of Kentucky, which had won statehood in 1792. As a result, Virginia officials were not interested in paying the debts Clark had taken on to supply his men while fighting for Kentucky and the Northwest Territory. In 1792, the Virginia legislature officially rejected these claims, leaving George Rogers Clark alone to face his creditors.

While his brother struggled with sickness and alcoholism, William Clark rode from town to town on the frontier to argue, plead, and negotiate. He met with angry merchants, many of whom were themselves facing bankruptcy because of the loans they had extended to George Rogers Clark. William attended court sessions to have judgments against his brother reduced and tried to settle disputes over land that George had seized during his campaigns. With the income from his properties, William Clark also helped pay some of his brother's debts, in return taking title to thousands of acres of wilderness that George Rogers Clark had claimed along the lower Ohio River.

These actions greatly helped his brother, but William Clark did not succeed on his own behalf. He did not have enough time or money to go into business for himself. His largest ambition at the time was the planning of a canal to be raised at the

Falls of the Ohio at Clarksville. When completed, the canal would allow river barges and keelboats to sail around the rough water at the falls, allowing Clark and his partners to earn money from tolls. Many such canals were operating successfully along the major rivers between the Great Lakes and the Atlantic Coast. But the Clarksville canal was never built. By the time a company was formed, William Clark was waiting to join Meriwether Lewis on an expedition that would put the United States into a race with the British for control of the Pacific Northwest.

4

RACING FOR THE NORTHWEST PASSAGE

M any people and nations dreamed of building a trading empire in the Northwest. The secretary of state of the United States, Thomas Jefferson, believed that his country would someday extend its territory beyond the Mississippi Valley, which formed the nation's western boundary.[1] But first, the United States would have to stake a claim to the land. Americans would have to explore it and map it. They would have to establish forts, trading posts, and settlements. They had to convince the Indians who lived there to stop trading with the British and to ally with the United States.

In 1792, the American captain Robert Gray had sailed north along the western coast of North

The idea of a western expedition to find the Northwest Passage was born in the mind of Thomas Jefferson.

America. In May, his ship dropped anchor just outside a wide bay. Although the ocean waves breaking at the bay's entrance threatened to wreck his ship, Gray pushed across them and sailed farther inland thirty-six miles. He discovered that the bay was actually an estuary—a body of water formed by a large river meeting the sea. Gray named this river after his ship, the *Columbia*. The estuary itself became known as Gray's Bay.

After leaving the Columbia's mouth, Gray sailed northward, meeting the British navigator George Vancouver. Intrigued by Gray's stories, Vancouver made an exploration of his own.[2] He sent a small boat under the command of Lieutenant William R. Broughton into Gray's Bay. Broughton sailed past the bay and up the Columbia a distance of one hundred miles. He spotted and named two high, snow-covered mountains: Mount Saint Helens and Mount Hood. On October 30, 1792, he claimed the entire Columbia River watershed—all the land drained by the river and its tributaries—for Great Britain.

By the next year, news of the discovery and the first exploration of the Columbia River had reached the United States. For years, people had dreamed of a direct water route across the American continent, which could serve traders and settlers. It was called the Northwest Passage. Thomas Jefferson believed that Gray's Bay and the lower Columbia River made up the final, westernmost part of the Northwest Passage. No nation had yet found or claimed the rest of the passage. The time had come for the United States to make the attempt.

Several American explorers, including Lieutenant John Armstrong and John Ledyard, had already set out to find the Northwest Passage. All had failed for lack of supplies, accurate maps, and preparation. Jefferson would try again. He asked the members of the American Philosophical Society in Philadelphia to support a new expedition. The society's members

After sailing one hundred miles past Gray's Bay, William Broughton spotted Mount Hood, pictured here, and Mount Saint Helens.

included the leading naturalists, philosophers, and geographers in the United States. Several of them, including President George Washington, agreed to help pay the expenses of the voyage.

Jefferson had many requests from men hoping to lead the expedition. Among them was the eighteen-year-old Virginian eager for adventure and fame: Meriwether Lewis. Jefferson knew and admired the Lewis family, who lived near his own estate in Albemarle County, Virginia.[3] But at the time he received Lewis's letter, he thought that Meriwether Lewis was too young and inexperienced.[4] Instead, he chose André Michaux, a French scientist who was living in the United States.

Michaux received his written instructions from Jefferson in the spring of 1793.[5] He was to travel up the Missouri River, cross the western mountains, find the Columbia, and then follow that river to its mouth. He would note the conditions of soil and collect plant specimens. He must learn as much as possible about the western tribes, and search for animal species Jefferson believed might inhabit the mountains, including llamas and mammoths (prehistoric elephants that were, in fact, extinct).

In June 1793, André Michaux set out for the Mississippi valley. He sailed down the Ohio River, stopping at the estate of George Rogers Clark. With Clark's advice and information, Michaux prepared

Early Attempts to Cross the Continent

Thomas Jefferson had long dreamed of an expedition to the Pacific Coast. Before his term as president, he made several attempts to carry out this dream.

In 1783, Jefferson asked George Rogers Clark to undertake an expedition to the Pacific, but Clark turned Jefferson down.

Three years later, in Paris, Jefferson met John Ledyard, an adventurer from Connecticut. Ledyard planned to travel across Russia and Siberia, and then sail to Alaska. From there he would proceed to the Mississippi valley. With only two dogs for company, Ledyard started out from Paris. He reached St. Petersburg on March 19. But that summer, he was stopped in Siberia by the Russian police. Suspected of being a spy, he was arrested, brought to Poland, and then released.

Secretary of War Henry Knox tried one more expedition in 1790. Knox hired Lieutenant John Armstrong to make an exploration up the Missouri River. But the overconfident Armstrong did not bother to prepare. He carried little spare food and no trading goods. He called a halt to the journey at Ste. Genevieve, on the eastern bank of the Mississippi.

to continue downstream to the junction of the Ohio and Mississippi rivers. But before the summer was over, Jefferson and President George Washington learned that Michaux was actually an agent of the French government. His secret orders were to raise a force to stir up trouble in the Spanish territory of Louisiana, which lay west of the Mississippi.

Jefferson ordered the expedition ended, and France ordered Michaux to leave the United States.

The Louisiana Territory

At the same time, a young military officer named Napoleon Bonaparte was rising to power in France. Like the British, Napoleon sought to extend his nation's territory in North America.[6] In 1800, after forcing Spain to accept his own brother as its king, Napoleon had the Spanish government sign the Treaty of San Ildefonso. By this agreement, France reclaimed the Louisiana Territory, which covered land west of the Mississippi all the way to the source of the river's western tributaries. To back up this claim, Napoleon would send a French force to New Orleans, the port near the Mississippi's mouth on the Gulf of Mexico. This army would protect Louisiana against the British and intimidate the United States. France would control traffic on the Mississippi, build its own trading empire, and expel any settlers who crossed the Mississippi from the United States.

French control of Louisiana greatly worried Thomas Jefferson, who had been elected president of the United States in 1800. Jefferson knew that the United States, Great Britain, and France could end up fighting over Louisiana and the Great Plains.[7] Napoleon also threatened American trade along the

Mississippi River to the port of New Orleans. To settle the crisis without war, Jefferson made plans to buy New Orleans from France.

Jefferson still held to the idea of a western expedition. The French were not yet in New Orleans, and the United States still had a good chance to find and claim a route to the Pacific. He only had to convince Congress to support the expedition and find the right commander to lead it. In fact, Jefferson believed he already had the expedition's leader at his side in the President's House in Washington, D.C. In February 1801, soon after his inauguration, the president had written to Meriwether Lewis to ask the young officer to serve as his personal secretary.

Planning the Western Expedition

After journeying three weeks from Pittsburgh, Meriwether Lewis reached Washington on April 1, 1801. He was soon working with Jefferson on many different kinds of official business. He attended meetings and ate meals with the president and his guests. He greeted the hundreds of foreign diplomats and politicians who came to call. He wrote letters, handled the president's documents, and served as Jefferson's personal messenger to Congress.

Lewis ably carried out his many assignments and earned the complete trust of the president. But

Jefferson did not hire Lewis for secretarial duties alone. The president believed Lewis might be ready to lead the western expedition, if such an expedition were still possible. While living under the same roof, and working with Lewis every day, Jefferson could plan the journey and make sure that Lewis was the best man available for the mission.[8]

Just after taking office, Jefferson had read a book called *Voyages from Montreal, on the River St. Lawrence, Through the Continent of North America, to the Frozen and Pacific Ocean, in the Years 1789 and 1793.* It was written by the British explorer Alexander Mackenzie, who had reached the Pacific Coast overland from Canada. The book demonstrated that the United States had no time to lose. Following the plan outlined by Mackenzie, the British would soon be moving across the continent to claim the rivers and ports of the Northwest Passage. The North West Company, or some other British company, would establish a settlement on the Pacific Ocean and seize control of the western fur trade.

Working together in the President's House, Jefferson and Lewis carefully discussed and planned the expedition. They kept the expedition as secret as necessary. (Because the land Lewis would cross west of the Mississippi River was still foreign territory, news of a planned American expedition there might cause a diplomatic—or military—conflict.) Jefferson would have to convince Congress to appropriate the money for the expedition. If Congress approved the expense, Lewis would work out the details and a timetable. He would also choose a second-in-command. It had to be a man he knew well and trusted, someone who could lead the expedition safely home in case of Lewis's death.

Lewis had again asked for the command of the western expedition. By this time, Jefferson was convinced of Lewis's ability.[9] Meanwhile, Jefferson tried to convince the Spanish that he was planning only scientific research. Although France now owned the Louisiana Territory, a Spanish governor still controlled Louisiana from the territorial capital of St. Louis. In the fall of 1802, Jefferson spoke with a Spanish ambassador named Carlos Martinez de Yrujo. He asked if Spain would oppose a scientific exploration of the Missouri River. Suspicious, Martinez warned the Spanish government that Jefferson's real purpose was to extend the territory of the United States to the Pacific Ocean.[10] Spain refused to grant Lewis a passport into Louisiana.

Jefferson and Lewis continued to prepare anyway. Lewis studied every book and map he could find on the Louisiana Territory, the Missouri River, and the Pacific Northwest. The president, a skilled amateur naturalist, gave Lewis lessons in geography, botany, biology, and astronomy. Lewis learned to use a navigational instrument called a sextant to calculate latitude and longitude along the journey. Lewis also studied reports on the American Indians of the Mississippi and Missouri valleys. An important part of his mission would be to meet the leaders of these tribes and ally them with the United States. Jefferson believed that a general peace among these tribes, in alliance with the United States, would allow his country to wrest control of trade from the British in the West.

On January 18, 1803, Jefferson delivered a secret message to Congress. In it, he asked Congress to approve money for an exploration of the territory west of the Mississippi River as far as the Pacific Ocean. On February 28, Congress approved Jefferson's proposal and agreed to spend twenty-five hundred dollars for supplies. At the same time, to avoid conflict with France in Louisiana, Jefferson was still attempting to buy the port of New Orleans. In early 1803, the president sent James Monroe, the governor of Virginia, to Paris to help Ambassador Robert Livingston negotiate the purchase. Congress would allow the diplomats to spend up to $9.375 million for the port.

Napoleon Bonaparte, the French leader, considered the offer again. Yellow fever was destroying the French Army on the Caribbean island of San

Domingo. This force would never occupy Louisiana, nor would it be able to fight France's greatest rival, Great Britain, in North America.[11] To keep the British from seizing the French claim in the New World, he decided to sell the entire Louisiana Territory to the United States for $15 million—about three cents an acre. "The sale assures forever the power of the United States," Napoleon said. "I have given England a rival who, sooner or later, will humble her pride."[12]

When the transfer became official, the entire Missouri River route as far as the eastern slopes of the Rocky Mountains would lie within the territory of the United States. Lewis would be the first to explore the western boundaries of that territory. His expedition would blaze a trail for the trappers, explorers, pioneers, and settlers who would follow him across the Mississippi River and to the Pacific Ocean.

The Two Captains

Lewis spent several weeks in Philadelphia, learning from the nation's leading geographers, doctors, and scientists. He bought a chronometer (an accurate and portable timepiece) that would help him compute longitude (a measure of distances west and east). He also gathered ribbons, knives, beads, fishhooks, paint, and other goods to trade with the Indian tribes of the Great Plains and the Rocky

The Pursuit of Lewis and Clark

The real purpose of the Lewis and Clark expedition was widely known by the time it started in 1804. Louisiana was now part of the United States, and France and Great Britain could do nothing to stop the captains. But Spain, which had colonies to the south, saw the expedition as a serious threat. The Spanish governors of these lands sent four parties north to search for and capture Lewis and Clark.

But the Spanish knew as little of the northern Rocky Mountains as did the Americans. None of the Spanish parties came close to the Corps of Discovery. Another expedition, that of Zebulon Pike, was not so lucky. Traveling in what was then northern New Spain (Mexico), Pike's party was arrested for trespassing by the Spanish and jailed. Eventually, Pike would be released, and the Mexican-American War would settle the ownership of New Mexico, Colorado, Utah, Arizona, and California.

Mountains. He purchased medicines from a pharmacist. He bought paper and ink, clothing, tobacco, and whiskey. Altogether, Lewis spent $2,324—most of the sum Congress had approved for the entire western expedition.[13]

By this time, Lewis had also decided on his co-commander. In the few months he had known

William Clark, Lewis had grown to admire Clark's toughness and leadership. Clark was a skilled mapmaker and boatman, he had dealt with tribes in the Northwest, and he also had talent as a frontier doctor. Clark's abilities would be useful to the expedition, and above all, he got along well with Meriwether Lewis.

Lewis prepared a letter to his friend, whom he had not seen since Clark's retirement from the army in 1796. Lewis described the planned western expedition. He detailed the many dangers as well as the rewards awaiting those who would join the Corps of Discovery, as he and Jefferson had named it, and see it through to the end. Lewis promised Clark a captain's commission as well as rank and pay equal to Lewis's own. At the end of the expedition, both men would receive a generous grant of land from the United States government. "If therefore there is anything under those circumstances, in this enterprise," Lewis wrote, "which would induce you to participate with me in it's fatiegues, it's dangers and it's honors, believe me there is no man on earth with whom I should feel equal pleasure in sharing them as with yourself."[14]

Clark received Lewis's letter on July 17, 1803. Frustrated by his business setbacks and as restless and ambitious as his younger friend, he wasted little time in considering Lewis's proposal. The next day, he wrote his reply: "The enterprise &c. is Such as I have long anticipated and am much pleased with—and as my situation in life will admit of my absence the length of time necessary to accomplish such an undertaking I will chearfully join you."[15]

The two men planned to meet that summer at the Falls of the Ohio.

5

DOWN THE OHIO, UP THE MISSOURI

Meriwether Lewis had worked out a rough timetable for the western expedition. In the spring of 1803, he would sail down the Ohio River from Pittsburgh. After picking up William Clark and the volunteers Clark had gathered at the Falls of the Ohio, Lewis would continue downstream to the Mississippi River. After reaching St. Louis, the captains would choose the final party and proceed up the Missouri River before winter weather froze the river and the northern plains. They would make a winter camp, cross the Rockies the next spring, find and follow the Columbia River to its mouth, and return to Washington, D.C., in late 1804.

On June 20, Jefferson made out his final instructions to Meriwether Lewis.[1] Lewis would take measurements of latitude and longitude, which would help geographers fix the position of the Missouri tributaries and the borders of the Louisiana Territory. He would seek out Indian tribes living on the plains and in the mountains, learn their languages and customs, and ally them with the United States. He would take samples of soil and plants, note the climate, search for animals unknown to science, and prospect for minerals. Along with the instructions, Jefferson ordered that Lewis be given open letters of credit.[2] With these letters, the president gave Lewis the authority to spend as much as he needed to resupply the expedition. The government would, eventually, make the necessary payments.

Setting Off

On July 15, Lewis reached Pittsburgh, his setting-off point. His first order of business was to write a short letter to Jefferson before inspecting the expedition's fifty-five-foot keelboat, which he had designed himself.[3] But on arriving at the river docks, he found that work on the boat had hardly begun. The boatwright, whom Lewis had hired without meeting, was spending much of his time drinking and arguing with his crew. Instead of setting off

Latitude and Longitude

Jefferson wanted an accurate map of the West. He instructed Lewis to take readings of latitude and longitude at every important landmark along the way.

Measuring latitude—distance north from the earth's equator—was fairly easy. Lewis would use a sextant to measure the height of the sun above the horizon at noon. Charts gave the correct measurement for each degree of latitude. Lewis would compare his measurement with those given in the charts to calculate his latitude.

Longitude measured distance in the other direction—west and east. Lewis also used a sextant to measure longitude. He would measure the angle between the moon and certain bright stars, then write down these measurements. The measurements would be compared with those at Greenwich, England, for the same time. The difference between the two measurements would allow a calculation of the distance west from Greenwich, in degrees of longitude.

down the Ohio immediately, Lewis would have to wait—possibly for weeks. There were no other boats, or shipyards, available.

While he waited, Lewis wrote to Clark, asking him to raise a company of worthy recruits and find a skilled hunter. The expedition would also need a translator and a guide. Clark had reported that many men were already volunteering for the Corps of Discovery. "I have had many applications from stout likely fellows," he wrote, "but have refused to retain some & put others off with a promis of giveing an answer after I see or hered from you . . ."[4] In Pittsburgh, Lewis had rounded up eleven volunteers of his own, including a river pilot, three volunteers for the western expedition, and seven soldiers to escort the keelboat down the Ohio River.

Meanwhile, Lewis waited, argued with the Pittsburgh boatwright, and lost time. The keelboat was finally ready on August 31, six weeks after Lewis had arrived in Pittsburgh. On the same morning, Lewis ordered men and supplies into the boat and gave the order to shove off. With a smaller pirogue (rowboat) trailing behind the keelboat, Meriwether Lewis set off down the Ohio River, bound for the Mississippi River and points west.

Meeting of the Captains

It was a year of drought, and in several places the river's shallows forced the keelboat aground. Where sandbars or driftwood blocked the channels, Lewis and the crew had to climb out of the boat and pull or push it into deeper water, or simply lift it past the obstructions. At Wheeling, in what is now West

Virginia, Lewis bought another pirogue and gathered supplies he had sent ahead from Harpers Ferry. Valuable weeks had been lost, however, and Lewis realized he would not be sailing up the Missouri River before winter set in.[5] With Clark, he would have to find a winter camp near St. Louis.

On October 15, 1803, the boats reached the Falls of the Ohio, where Clark was waiting with several volunteers. Lewis and Clark, meeting for the first time since their days together in the Chosen Rifle Company, talked over their plans. They checked supplies and reviewed the volunteers, rejecting more than one hundred men and finally settling on nine. Clark's slave, York, whom he had inherited from his father, would also join the Corps of Discovery.

On October 26, the three boats again set off downriver. On November 11, the expedition stopped for a few days at Fort Massac, thirty miles from the mouth of the Ohio. There, Lewis and Clark hired a hunter and scout named George Drouillard. Son of a French-Canadian father and a Shawnee mother, Drouillard knew American Indian sign language, as well as French and English, and could serve the expedition as an interpreter. Lewis sent Drouillard to gather eight volunteers at South West Point, a fort in Tennessee.

After Fort Massac, the boats turned north, out of the Ohio and into the powerful currents of the Mississippi River. The captains carefully guided the boats from one side of the river to the other, searching for calm water where oaring and poling could overcome the current. At Fort Kaskaskia, on the river's eastern bank in Indiana Territory, they picked up more recruits. While Lewis went ahead on horseback to St. Louis, Clark stayed with the boats.

On December 8, Lewis rode into St. Louis to meet Carlos Delassus, the Spanish governor who would rule Louisiana until the formal transfer of the territory from Spain to France, and then to the United States, took place. On instructions from the Spanish government, Delassus would not give permission for the expedition to pass to the west bank of the Mississippi. Instead, he said that Lewis and Clark would have to wait until a formal ceremony could be held in the spring, officially transferring Louisiana to the United States.

William Clark had scouted out a proper campsite at the mouth of the Riviere Dubois, or Wood River. The site occupied land on the east bank of the Mississippi, opposite the mouth of the Missouri. The company built cabins, supply huts, and a fence. Lewis and Clark named their new outpost Camp Wood. They now had the entire winter to prepare the Corps of Discovery.

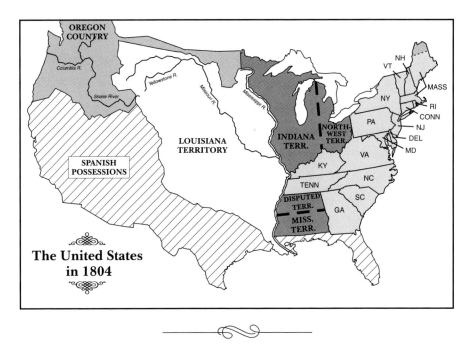

OREGON
COUNTRY

Columbia R.

Yellowstone R.

Snake River

Missouri R.

Mississippi R.

LOUISIANA
TERRITORY

SPANISH
POSSESSIONS

INDIANA
TERR.

NORTH-
WEST
TERR.

NH
VT

MASS

NY

RI
CONN

PA

NJ
DEL

VA

MD

KY

TENN

NC

DISPUTED
TERR.

SC

GA

MISS.
TERR.

**The United States
in 1804**

*This map shows the United States as it looked in 1804, at the time
of the addition of the Louisiana Purchase.*

Against the Current

At Camp Wood, Lewis and Clark carefully observed
their volunteers. The men selected to follow the
captains west would have to be in excellent health.
They also had to bear up under the boredom and
petty squabbles of camp life. In March 1804, the
captains finally settled on twenty-five men, several
of whom possessed useful talents and knowledge.[6]
John Shields was a skilled gunsmith and an excellent
shot. Patrick Gass knew carpentry, while William

Warner could cook for a large company. The Corps of Discovery was divided into three squads, with three of the men appointed sergeants: Charles Floyd, Nathaniel Pryor, and John Ordway. Each of the sergeants would be responsible for a squad. On the captains' orders, each would also have to keep a personal journal of the voyage.

In early May, Captain Lewis had bad news for Clark. The War Department would not issue Clark a captain's commission, because there were no places available. Clark would have to serve as a lieutenant. Lewis intended the two men to share command. "I think it will be best to let none of our party or any other persons know any thing about the grade," Lewis wrote to Clark.[7] The two men would have equal authority and equal pay. To the members of the expedition, they would both be captains.

Two months earlier, in March, a ceremony in St. Louis had marked the transfer of the Louisiana Territory from Spain to France. For one day, the French flag flew over the city. On the next day, France formally transferred the territory to the United States. The way to the Rocky Mountains was now clear for Lewis and Clark.

As the weather warmed, the company prepared the keelboat and the two pirogues for launching. A company of ten French oarsmen would row one of the pirogues, while the other would carry a company of six regular army volunteers. Under the command of Corporal Richard Warfington, these six soldiers would escort the expedition as far as its next winter quarters. The keelboat carried the twenty-nine permanent members of the expedition, which included York, Drouillard, Captains Lewis and Clark, three sergeants, and twenty-two enlisted privates. This party would continue to the Pacific and back.

On May 14, Clark set out across the Mississippi and into the Missouri River. In six days, he reached St. Charles, where Lewis had ridden ahead to meet the party. There, the captains hired Pierre Cruzatte and Francis Labiche, who would serve as translators and guides along the route. On May 21, the expedition left St. Charles, pointing the three boats into the powerful current of the Missouri River. That day, with the men straining at the oars, the Corps of Discovery traveled a little over three miles upstream.

Meeting the Oto

Each evening, the commanders scouted the river and its banks for a good campsite. The low, sandy islands in the river offered the most protection. After making camp, the company posted two sentries—one on the land side, if they camped ashore, and the other always near the keelboat. In the morning, the commanders sent men ashore to hunt for game. Along the lower Missouri, hunters never had to stray far from the river, because the country held plenty of deer, elk, black bear, and buffalo. The men also caught fish—sometimes hundreds at a time—in the river and its tributaries.

The divided command worked well. Lewis and Clark had different abilities, and each carried out a vital role. Clark, the better river pilot, took responsibility for guiding the boats. He also kept notes for a map that he planned to complete after the expedition returned home. Clark served as the expedition's doctor, treating both whites and Indians with medicines prepared by Benjamin Rush. Lewis, with his training in astronomy, botany, and zoology, often left the keelboat to tramp over the countryside. He gathered many plant and animal specimens, examined rocks and soil, and took precise

Benjamin Rush prepared the medicines used by Lewis and Clark to treat the sick during the expedition.

Meeting Dr. Benjamin Rush

Meriwether Lewis knew that preparations for the voyage must include medical supplies. He would be spending more than a year in the wilderness, far from any doctors. An important part of his preparation in Philadelphia was spent with Dr. Benjamin Rush.

Rush made up a list of needed medicines and gave Lewis advice. Rush also offered a pill of his own invention, nicknamed the "Thunderbolt" or the "Thunderclapper."[8] The pill contained calomel (a mixture of mercury and chlorine) and the dried roots of the jalap plant. The pills cured constipation—almost immediately. On Rush's advice, Lewis also bought opium, mercury, Epsom salts, powdered bark, powdered rhubarb, herb powders, pills, and medical instruments. Some of the medicines were used often, others hardly at all. But the one item in the expedition's medicine chest that the members never forgot were "Rush's Thunderbolts."

measurements from the stars to determine his position.

In late July, the Corps of Discovery reached the mouth of the Platte River. In the nearby plains, George Drouillard encountered a band of Oto, the first American Indians to be met by the expedition. Lewis invited the Oto to a council, which took place on the Missouri's sandy banks on August 3. While the Oto chiefs watched, the Corps of Discovery raised the American flag along the riverbank. Lewis and Clark paraded their men and offered each of the chiefs gifts and tokens of friendship from the government of the United States. Through his interpreters, Lewis gave a long speech, announcing that a new nation, led by a Great Father in the East (the president of the United States), now ruled the Missouri River and the plains. The captain asked the chiefs to "live in peace with all the white men." Lewis also used threats: "Your great father, the great chief of the Seventeen great nations [states] of America . . . could consume you as the fire consumes the grass of the plains." If they followed his advice, he promised, "You will then obtain goods on much better terms than you have ever received them heretofore."[9]

The council with the Oto went well, and Lewis felt certain that he had made a new ally for the United States. But soon afterward, the Corps of Discovery began suffering bad luck.

On August 17, Drouillard brought in Private Moses Reed, who had deserted with his rifle. The captains held a court-martial, finding Reed guilty and drumming him out of the expedition. Reed was demoted to one of the pirogues and would have to stay behind when the expedition made its winter

The expedition met different tribes along the way and offered them gifts and tokens of friendship.

camp. On August 19, Sergeant Floyd suffered a sudden, mysterious, and violent illness. The captains had no medicine to heal Floyd, who probably had a ruptured appendix, and the sergeant died two days later. After his burial, the company took a vote and elected Patrick Gass to replace Floyd as a sergeant and squad leader. Floyd was the first United States soldier to die west of the Mississippi, and Gass became the first man to win an election in the West.

To the Mandan Villages

During the next week, the expedition met the Yankton band of Sioux. The captains again offered presents, and Lewis repeated the speech he had delivered to the Oto. On August 30, Lewis and Clark named five of the Yankton official chiefs. This practice made it easier for the United States to negotiate with the different tribes, although the Yankton themselves, like most American Indian tribes, did not "elect" permanent leaders. On September 23, in what is now central South Dakota, the expedition encountered the Teton Sioux.

Although the Yankton had been friendly, the carefully planned speeches and gifts did not appease the Teton. They controlled trade along this section of the river, and they decided who would pass through their lands. They would not give up their authority to this small group of white men, or to an invisible Great Father. After inspecting the keelboat, one of the Sioux leaders, called the Partisan, angrily seized the boat's towline and declared that the Corps of Discovery would not pass. Men on both sides prepared their weapons. Clark ordered the keelboat's large swivel gun ready to fire.

The tense situation ended with strong words and a further gift of tobacco from Lewis. Black Buffalo, one of the Sioux leaders, talked the Partisan into letting the expedition pass. Although the expedition was able to proceed, the co-commanders had discovered that among the Sioux, as with most American Indian bands, authority was divided. Dealing with them would take careful diplomacy and a show of force. Distributing presents, making speeches, and choosing chiefs would not be enough to win the friendship of the Teton Sioux or of many other tribes.

For the next month, the expedition sailed northward and around the Missouri River's sharp, looping bends. In late October, Lewis and Clark met the Mandan Indians, who lived in a group of permanent villages along the river. Snow was beginning to fall, and the nights were freezing. The captains decided to search the nearby plains for a suitable winter camp. After a long hike along the banks, Clark found a good site opposite the mouth of the Knife River, in what is now central North Dakota. The men began cutting cottonwood trees and raising two lines of huts, as well as officers' quarters and a smokehouse. A barred gate and a fence of cottonwood logs stuck upright in the ground completed Fort Mandan.

The company spent several months camped near the Mandan and the Hidatsa, a neighboring tribe. In need of food, Lewis and Clark traded gifts and goods for bushels of corn. The company's blacksmith, John Shields, forged knives and axes to trade. A

In late October, Lewis and Clark set up winter camp near a Mandan village along the Missouri River.

rusted stove was taken apart, piece by piece, and traded to the Mandan, who made knives and arrowheads from the iron. To celebrate Christmas, the men fired off a few rounds, and Lewis distributed an extra ration of whiskey. Late into the night, the men danced while Pierre Cruzatte played the fiddle. In his journal, Sergeant Ordway noted: "we had the Best to eat that could be had, & continued firing dancing & frolicking dureing the whole day . . . We enjoyed a merry cristmas dureing the day & evening untill nine oClock—all in peace & quietness."[10]

6

END OF THE EXPEDITION

With the first signs of spring in 1805, the Corps of Discovery prepared to resume its journey up the Missouri. Using the trunks of cottonwood trees, the men built six dugout canoes that would help them to navigate the shallower waters ahead. In the meantime, Lewis carefully packed his mineral, plant, and animal specimens into the keelboat for the trip back downstream to St. Louis. Among many other objects, he had collected antelopes, a hare, ram's horns, buffalo robes, samples of tobacco, a Mandan pot, fox skins, magpies, and a new discovery: a prairie dog.[1] Although President Jefferson had also asked Lewis to send his journals back, Lewis decided to keep them. They were the single most valuable item he carried, and he did not want to risk losing them should anything happen to Corporal Warfington's crew and the keelboat.

That winter, Lewis and Clark had hired a French-Canadian interpreter named Toussaint Charbonneau, whose wife, a Shoshone named Sacagawea, would also join the company. Her infant son, Jean-Baptiste Charbonneau, had been born at Fort Mandan with Lewis's help. Farther upriver, Sacagawea would help Lewis and Clark buy horses from the Shoshone, to use in crossing the Rocky Mountains.

The Gates of the Mountains

On April 7, the expedition resumed. In a short time, Lewis and Clark passed into unmapped territory. In the surrounding countryside grazed large, wild herds of buffalo, elk, and antelopes. After passing the mouth of the Yellowstone River, the company began to encounter grizzly bears. Lewis boasted: "the Indians may well fear this anamal equiped as they generally are with their bows and arrows . . . but in the hands of skillfull riflemen they are by no means as formidable or dangerous as they have been represented."[2] But the captains soon learned to fear the big bears. On May 5, Clark wrote, "I went out with one man . . . and Killed the bear, which was

The Birth of Pomp

Lewis had a chance to put his doctoring talents to use in the winter of 1811. On February 11, Sacagawea went into painful labor. Unsure of what to do, Lewis asked for advice. The trader René Jessaume mentioned that some Indians believed the rattle of the rattlesnake was effective in bringing on a birth.

Lewis happened to have just such a rattle with him. He broke it up, put it in some water, and gave it to Sacagawea to drink. He wrote in his journal that within ten minutes, she gave birth to the baby.

Toussaint Charbonneau, the husband of Sacagawea, named his new son Jean-Baptiste. But William Clark invented a nickname of his own—Pomp—for the youngest member of the Corps of Discovery.

verry large and a turrible looking animal, which we found verry hard to kill. we Shot ten Balls into him before we killed him."[3] On the next day, Lewis admitted in his journal that "I find that the curiosity of our party is pretty well satisfyed with rispect to this anamal . . ."[4] From that point on, the party avoided grizzlies whenever possible.

On May 26, the distant Rocky Mountains finally came into view—the first sighting of the mountains by white Americans. "I felt a secret pleasure," wrote Lewis, "in finding myself so near the head of the heretofore conceived boundless Missouri."[5] The river was running faster and shallower, and the plains were giving way to gently rolling hills and steep bluffs. Lewis and Clark watched for signs of the great waterfall described by the Hidatsa tribe. On June 2, the party came to the puzzling fork at Marias River. On June 12, while walking ahead of the boats, Lewis discovered the Great Falls of the Missouri River. The river narrowed further, with steep cliffs replacing the sloping banks.

Sheer stone walls rose along the riverbanks at a place Lewis named the Gates of the Mountains. Autumn was approaching, and the expedition had only reached the eastern foothills of the Rocky Mountains. Lewis and Clark knew they must reach the Shoshone and trade for horses before the snows blocked their passage. Sacagawea pointed out landmarks to the captains and found the spot where she had been captured by a Hidatsa raiding party many years before.

In mid-August, Lewis and Clark reached the Continental Divide, in what is now western Montana. Here, the rivers began to run west to the Pacific. Instead of finding the western slope of the Rocky Mountains, and perhaps the Columbia River itself, the captains saw a series of high, snowbound ridges that stretched to the western horizon. This was hardly a short, fast route to the Pacific Ocean.

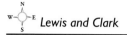

Lewis named this place the Gates of the Mountains because of the steep stone walls that rose above the riverbank.

Instead, it was the steep Bitterroot Range of the Rocky Mountains, and the Columbia was nowhere in sight.

On the other side of the Divide lived a band of Shoshone. By sheer coincidence, this band happened to be led by Cameahwait, the brother of Sacagawea. After reaching the Shoshone camp, Lewis sent Clark ahead to find the best route over the mountains and into the Columbia watershed. As described by the Shoshone, a trail to the north through the Bitterroots would lead them to a tributary of the Columbia. The

Sacagawea often served as an interpreter for Lewis and Clark when they encountered Indians.

co-commanders traded tools, knives, and articles of clothing for thirty horses, made up smaller packs, and prepared to cross the high mountains. A Shoshone guide, whom they had nicknamed Old Toby, would lead them.

In the Columbia Valley

Rain, sleet, and snow fell as the expedition struggled along the steep trails. With little food, and no game at this elevation, Lewis and Clark were running out of time. After crossing a river that Lewis named Clark's River (later changed to the Bitterroot River), they reached the Lolo Pass and then a village of the Nez Percé tribe, led by a chief named Twisted Hair. Lewis branded the horses and left them with the Nez Percé, who promised to keep them until the party returned from the Pacific. Guided downstream by Twisted Hair, the expedition reached the Clearwater River, then the Snake. On October 16, Lewis and Clark struck the Columbia River. It was much too late to return before winter. The Corps of Discovery would have to find a winter camp on the Pacific.

The rivers on the western side of the Continental Divide traveled a much shorter distance to the sea.

Lewis and Clark encountered at least four hundred Salish Indians at Clark's River.

They ran faster, and several times dangerous rapids overturned the canoes. But Lewis and Clark were in a hurry to reach the ocean. Instead of portaging, they ran most of the rapids. After the turbulent Cascades, about one hundred miles upstream from the river's mouth, the expedition entered a wide, calm estuary—Gray's Bay. Here, the waters of the Columbia River rose and fell with the ocean tide. The Pacific Ocean had to be near.

A fierce, cold rainstorm came up. For eight days, a strong wind blew inland, forcing the expedition to camp along the narrow ledges of the bay. The captains decided to cross the estuary to search for a better campsite. On the south side of the Columbia, they found a good clearing along the Netul River.[6] On Christmas Day, 1805, the Corps of Discovery moved into its winter quarters, which the captains named Fort Clatsop, after the Clatsop tribe. That evening, the expedition prepared a Christmas meal of boiled elk, roots, and fish.

The fort lay close to herds of elk and deer that would provide enough meat to sustain the expedition members until spring. But the rain and humidity along the coast made life miserable. The men could not keep their campfires burning or their clothes dry. They could not operate a smokehouse to preserve their meat. The party survived on dog

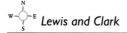

After running the turbulent Cascades of the Columbia River, the expedition entered Gray's Bay and then set up winter camp at Fort Clatsop.

meat, whale blubber, and roots, and traded nearly the last of their goods to the Chinook tribe for food.

Lewis and Clark discovered that these Indians already knew a few words of English. Lewis learned that British ships arrived here from time to time to trade. When asked where the ships came from, the Chinook pointed to the southwest—the general direction of the British-controlled Hawaiian Islands. At some time, and probably soon, one of these ships would leave behind people as well as goods. British colonists and fur traders would arrive to begin settling the Pacific Northwest.

The Return Journey

On March 23, 1806, the captains gave the order to prepare the boats and strike camp. Before he left, Lewis posted a sign that listed the names of the members of the expedition and announced that the United States had reached the Pacific Coast by way of the Rocky Mountains. It would be the first American claim to the Pacific Northwest.

During the winter, no ships had arrived at the Columbia's mouth.[7] The expedition would have to row, ride, and walk back across the Rockies and follow the Missouri downstream to St. Louis. Lewis hurried the boats back up the Columbia, intending to collect his horses from the Nez Percé and cross the mountains during the early summer. The captains had to reach the Nez Percé camp before the tribe left for the annual buffalo hunt on the Great Plains.

At the rapids of the Cascades, the men managed to haul the boats upstream with the use of tow ropes. At the Umatilla River, the expedition reached a village of the Walla Walla tribe. The Walla Walla described a direct route to the Clearwater River that would allow the expedition to avoid the steep canyons and bends of the Snake River. The shortcut

Making Salt

For more than a year, the Lewis and Clark expedition lived on broiled, boiled, and dried meat. The meat was often stringy and tasteless; a pinch of salt gave it its only flavor. But by the time they reached the Pacific Ocean, Lewis and Clark were out of salt.

This is one reason the captains decided to make their winter camp near the ocean, where seawater could be converted to salt. Seawater was boiled in large copper kettles. The water, after evaporating, left a film of salt on the inside of the kettles. The men scraped off the salt and collected it in leather pouches.

The site of the Lewis and Clark saltworks is now a part of the Fort Clatsop National Memorial in Oregon.

allowed Lewis and Clark to reach the Nez Percé in good time. But the expedition had arrived at the Bitterroots too early—deep snow still blocked the mountain passes.

In early June, Lewis lost patience. Although the Nez Percé warned him of the snowbound, slippery trails ahead, he decided to try to cross the high mountain passes. On June 15, with sixty-six horses carrying supplies, the expedition set out from their camp on Weippe Prairie. Fallen timber blocked the trails; the horses and men stumbled through deep snowbanks. On June 17, Lewis and Clark ordered a retreat—the first and last of the entire expedition. They waited at Hungry Creek, a few miles back down the trail, and sent a detachment back to the Nez Percé to find guides. On June 24, they set out again. This time, the melting snowbanks allowed a passage to Traveler's Rest in the Bitterroot valley, where the expedition halted for two days.

At Traveler's Rest, the captains decided to divide the expedition. Lewis would continue directly east, along the Blackfoot River, to the Great Falls. He would follow the Missouri to the Marias River, then follow that stream north to find its source. Clark would continue along the route the party had followed the year before. At the Jefferson River, he would pick up the canoes and supplies left behind. Clark would then select a small party under Sergeant Ordway to sail down the Missouri. With the canoes, Ordway would meet Lewis and his party at the mouth of the Marias River. Clark would proceed overland to the Yellowstone River, then sail downriver to meet Lewis at the junction of the Yellowstone and the Missouri.

Encounter with the Blackfeet

On July 3, with a party of nine men, Lewis started out. Fearing the hostile Blackfeet who roamed the plains ahead, the Nez Percé guides had turned back to their village. At the Great Falls, Lewis left a squad of six men to wait for Sergeant Ordway. He continued on with Drouillard and Joseph and Reubin Field. On July 26, while near the Two Medicine River, Lewis spotted a small party of eight Blackfeet. Outnumbered, Lewis decided to advance for a meeting rather than flee.

Through Drouillard's sign language, Lewis explained to the Blackfeet warriors that he was the commander of a much larger, armed party that was close by. After distributing gifts, he invited the Blackfeet to camp with him that night. The warriors seemed friendly, but early the next morning, the angry shouts of Drouillard and the Field brothers woke Lewis. The Blackfeet had seized a rifle and were now struggling with the white men. Suddenly, two of the Blackfeet went running out of the camp. The Field brothers gave chase. Reubin Field caught up with one of the Blackfeet and after a short struggle stabbed the Indian. Lewis chased two others to the base of a cliff. A bullet whistled past Lewis's head; his own shot killed one of the Blackfeet.

Lewis ran back to the camp. He ordered his men to gather and burn the Blackfeet weapons and shields. Lewis also collected a rifle and four of the Blackfeet horses. Fearing an attack from a larger party, the four men rode hard for the Missouri River. Late that night, just after reaching the river, they spotted Sergeant Ordway's party rounding a bend and coming into view. Still in danger, Lewis immediately pushed downriver to meet Clark.

Return to St. Louis

Lewis had left two Blackfeet dead at the camp. Certain that the tribe was raising a war party to find the whites and revenge the killings, he made swift progress down the Missouri River, stopping only to hunt on the nearby plains. At the junction with the Yellowstone, Lewis found a written message from Clark. The message warned Lewis of scarce game and troublesome mosquitoes; Clark had pushed on from this spot with his own party. The two captains finally reunited on August 12.

From Clark, Lewis learned that members of the Crow tribe had raided Sergeant Pryor's party in the Yellowstone Valley. The horses under Pryor's guard had been stolen. Lewis and Clark had planned to trade these horses at the Mandan villages, in exchange for presents for the Sioux. Still hoping to bring the Sioux into an alliance with the United States, Lewis had planned to invite the Sioux chiefs to a council with President Jefferson in Washington. The theft of Pryor's horses ended this plan.

Two days later, the expedition reached the Mandan villages. From this point, Lewis and Clark hoped for a quick and easy journey back to St.

Louis. They released John Colter, an expedition member who had asked permission to return up the Missouri River with two fur trappers. Toussaint Charbonneau, Sacagawea, and their young son, whom Clark had nicknamed Pomp, would remain at the Mandan villages. Before setting off from the Mandan, the captains took aboard Sheheke, or Big White, a Mandan chief who had agreed to visit Jefferson in Washington.

While rowing downstream through the Great Plains, the expedition met trappers and traders rowing north. They learned from these parties that many people had given up the members of the Corps of Discovery for lost, captured, or dead.[8] Anxious to relay word of the expedition to the president, Lewis prepared a letter for Clark to send ahead to Clark's brother in Kentucky. The co-captains knew the letter would be published in the Kentucky newspapers and then quickly reprinted in the East. This would be the fastest way for the two men to spread the news of their safe arrival in St. Louis.[9]

On September 23, 1806, a little over twenty-eight months after casting off from Camp Wood, the Lewis and Clark expedition rowed up to the docks of St. Louis. After quitting the boats, Lewis took a room in the home of Pierre Chouteau, a wealthy St. Louis fur trader, and began composing a letter to Jefferson. Lewis had bad news for the president: A barrier of high mountains, hundreds of miles wide, lay between the Louisiana Purchase and the Columbia watershed. The trails followed by Lewis and Clark would never serve as a useful transcontinental shipping route.[10] The Northwest Passage, which geographers and explorers had believed in and searched for ever since the European discovery of the New World, did not exist.

Despite this setback, Lewis and Clark had led a daring and successful exploration. They had lost only one man, to illness, and had met with several Indian tribes in the attempt to win them over to trade with the United States. Lewis had collected plant, animal, and rock specimens, many of them unknown to scientists. He had also recorded several tribal vocabularies. Clark had gathered information for a new, detailed map he would draw of the lands west of the Missouri River to the Pacific. Several volumes of journals and scientific notes had survived the long voyage. The captains were also bringing Big White, chief of the Mandan, to the nation's capital.

Lewis and Clark spent the next few days greeting well-wishers, attending dinners, and preparing for the journey back east. There would be endless discussions and explanations of the many discoveries they had made. Lewis began working out a plan to establish a series of government-operated fur posts along the route he had just blazed to the Pacific. To satisfy the public demand for information about the journey, he also began planning a three-volume edition of the diaries. On September 26, William Clark made the last entry in the captains' official journals: "a fine morning we commenced wrighting &c."[11]

7

MERIWETHER LEWIS AFTER THE EXPEDITION

———⟨∽⟩———

Meriwether Lewis reached Washington, D.C., on December 28, 1806. The capital proclaimed the thirty-two-year-old captain a hero for his daring exploits. He listened to speeches of praise in Congress and enthusiastic toasts at celebration dinners. Meanwhile, the president and Congress debated the rewards due the leaders and men of the expedition. They finally settled on a grant of sixteen hundred acres of land to each of the captains. Each of the privates and sergeants would receive double pay and three hundred twenty acres of land. Jefferson nominated Lewis as the new governor of the Louisiana Territory. Congress approved the appointment on March 9, 1807.

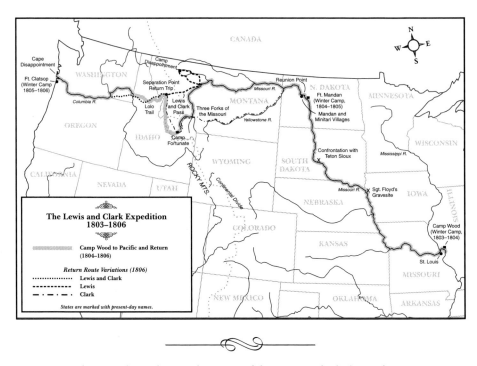

This map shows the complete route of the Lewis and Clark expedition.

Trouble in St. Louis

Jefferson made another important appointment for Louisiana: Frederick Bates would serve as secretary—or second-in-command—to Governor Lewis. When Lewis and Clark reappeared in St. Louis in 1806, Bates was serving as an associate judge in the Michigan Territory.[1] As long as Lewis remained in Washington, Bates was to govern the new territory and carry out, as best he could, Lewis's instructions. Bates's appointment, however, did not help Meriwether Lewis. Bates had no experience or skill in dealing with Indians or with the problems of the western frontier. Soon after arriving in the spring of 1807, he found himself overwhelmed by the job's many problems.[2]

While Lewis and Clark were searching for the Northwest Passage, St. Louis had grown quickly as the jumping-off point for western explorers and fur-trappers. The city was full of ambitious entrepreneurs eager for a chance to profit from the land and resources of the Louisiana Territory. Bates soon found his office serving as the battleground for their bitter disputes over land claims and trading privileges.

While in Washington, Lewis had made plans to win the western tribes to the United States by granting trading rights to cooperative tribes and withholding trade from those who stayed hostile. But in St. Louis, Bates's actions frustrated those plans. When British traders incited Indians to attack United States trading posts, Bates did nothing. When settlers living on the frontier north of St. Louis asked for arms to protect themselves, Bates refused to help them. The Missouri River country grew violent and chaotic. Indian raids on trading posts and settlements increased, while a tide of American settlers poured across the Mississippi, staking claim to land that the government sought to

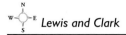

keep off-limits. Lewis and Clark's long and risky voyage to extend the borders of the United States began to look like an expensive failure.

Preparing the Journals

While Bates attended to duties in St. Louis, Lewis remained in the East, attending banquets, sitting for portraits, and making speeches. The adulation of the public and Congress was drawing him away from his appointment in Louisiana. His futile search for a wife might have depressed him; his bouts of late-night carousing with friends began to affect his judgment.

Through an understanding with both Jefferson and Clark, Lewis would direct the editing and publication of the expedition journals. But Lewis soon discovered that he was not alone in his publishing efforts. During the expedition, the sergeants had kept their own diaries, under orders from the co-captains. Now one of them, Patrick Gass, had arranged to publish his journals. Fearing competition from Gass's book, Lewis wrote a public notice criticizing Gass's qualifications as a naturalist: "He cannot . . . possibly give any accurate information on these subjects . . . and the whole which can be expected from his Journal is merely a limited detail of our daily transactions."[3] David McKeehan, publisher for Patrick Gass's proposed book, shot back a sarcastic reply: "It is to be regretted that the wealth and honors heaped upon you so soon rendered your heart callous toward the companions of your 'fatigues and painful sufferings'!"[4]

Lewis did not reply to McKeehan's letter. He began making arrangements for publication of his own work, hiring artists to create drawings of the flora and fauna he had discovered in the West. Dr. Benjamin Barton, a famous naturalist and philosopher, would edit the scientific notes. Lewis engaged a Philadelphia publisher, John Conrad, to bring out the book. Lewis himself wrote his book's prospectus, or advertisement, which was printed in July 1807, and promised, in part, "a narrative of the voyage with a description of the most remarkable places in those hitherto unknown wilds of America."[5]

The daily journals kept by Lewis and Clark covered more than twenty-eight months of exploration, conflict, discovery, and danger in an unknown land. There were hundreds of entries and many thousands of words. It would take a lot of hard work to prepare the material for the printer. Yet Lewis neglected the job and did not bother to hire an editor to do it for him. He kept the journals in his baggage, never bothering to open them and get to work. The drudgery of the task may have put him off; his busy schedule in Washington and Philadelphia, as well as his duties in St. Louis, may

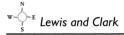

have distracted him. Lewis did not offer any explanation for the delay. Conrad, Jefferson, and the public would have to wait.

The Pryor Expedition

In St. Louis, under William Clark's direction, Nathaniel Pryor took command of an expedition to return Big White, the Mandan chief, to his home after his visit to the president. After meeting with Big White in Washington, President Jefferson had given this return voyage a top priority. The Mandan were an important ally, and the journey must succeed. On May 18, 1807, Pryor, Pierre Chouteau, and Big White set out up the Missouri River with a party of fourteen soldiers and twenty-two traders.

If there were to be any trouble, Pryor might well expect it from the Sioux, who had nearly ambushed Lewis and Clark's party in 1804. By September, Pryor had passed the mouth of the Platte River and reached the Great Plains. On September 9, he reached an Arikara village. As Lewis and Clark had done three years earlier, Pryor prepared to offer trading goods to smooth his passage through their lands.

But the Arikara were no longer peaceful. During the Lewis and Clark expedition, one of their chiefs had suffered a fatal illness while traveling among the white men to the East. Now the Arikara were suspicious and angry. When Pryor's group of white soldiers passed through their lands escorting one of their enemies, a Mandan chief, they attacked.

The Arikara swarmed around Pryor's boats with rifles, arrows, and knives. The soldiers and traders managed to beat back the attack, but three traders were killed and several soldiers suffered serious wounds. George Shannon, who had traveled to the Pacific and back with Lewis and Clark, would lose one of his legs. Pryor immediately retreated down the Missouri.[6]

The Pryor expedition had been a disaster. But Jefferson's promise to the Mandan had to be kept. Big White had to be returned to his people. As soon as Lewis arrived in St. Louis, he would have to try again.

Plans for the Louisiana Territory

In January 1808, Meriwether Lewis attended the wedding of William Clark and Julia Hancock. The next month, he finally set out for St. Louis. He arrived at his post on March 8, a full year after Congress had approved his appointment.

In the meantime, Lewis had been working on a new plan for the territory. By that summer, he had begun to carry it out.[7] First, the United States would take firm control of the land it had bought from France by making commercial and military

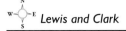

alliances with the tribes of the Louisiana Territory. With the help of the friendly Indians, the British traders would be driven north, out of United States territory, and back to the frozen portages of the Canadian fur route.

Then, a series of forts would be raised on the Missouri and along its most important tributaries. The forts would serve as protected government trading posts. Lewis himself would grant trading licenses. He would also try to prevent white settlement in lands ceded to American Indians. The Sioux and other hostile nations who allied with the British would be embargoed. No one would be permitted to buy their goods or sell to them. The loss of trade would, eventually, convince them to cooperate with the United States.

Unfortunately, affairs in Louisiana were not going according to plan. The troubles that had plagued Bates now became Lewis's problems. A group of Sauk and Fox were involved in the murder of a frontier settler. The British were stirring up trouble among the tribes of the upper Mississippi River valley, inciting them to raid white settlements. White settlers were refusing to move back East; in fact, hundreds were crossing the Mississippi every day to claim land in the Louisiana Territory. Traders were working without government licenses. The Louisiana militia, which had

Forts like this one were built along the Missouri River to protect government trading posts.

been placed under William Clark's command, was too small to keep the peace, and the United States Army, down to a small peacetime force of several thousand officers and enlisted men, was too small to serve in the Louisiana Territory as a frontier guard.

Nevertheless, like most Louisiana settlers, Lewis and Clark saw opportunity as well as hardship in this new land. In late 1808, the two explorers joined a group of St. Louis merchants in founding the Missouri River Fur Company. Manuel Lisa, a St. Louis trader, would direct the company. William Clark, Pierre Chouteau, and Meriwether Lewis's brother Reuben Lewis were among the partners. Meriwether Lewis participated as a secret partner, hoping to avoid the scandal that would come from his openly profiting from his actions as governor. The company began laying plans for its first order of business: the return of Big White to the Mandan.

The Chouteau Expedition

In February 1809, Lewis drew up a contract on behalf of the United States with the Missouri River Fur Company.[8] Lisa and his partners were to raise a force of 125 men and supply them with weapons. The company would hire boats and sail up the Missouri to the Mandan towns, where Big White would be returned. If this mission were accomplished, the government would pay the company seven thousand dollars. After reaching the Mandan towns, the company's traders would continue into the Yellowstone River fur country. Here, with an exclusive license granted by Lewis, they would be allowed to trap as many furs as they could return to the St. Louis market.

The government agreed to advance the company thirty-five hundred dollars to purchase supplies—one thousand dollars more than Congress had appropriated for the entire Lewis and Clark expedition. Nevertheless, Lewis still believed the company would need more trading goods as well as additional supplies to deal with the Arikara and the Cheyenne, who had joined the Arikara in their attempt to stop any upriver expeditions. Certain that the government would honor his debts, Lewis signed notes to pay for additional supplies of gifts and gunpowder.

Lewis gave Pierre Chouteau, who would lead the expedition, very specific instructions for dealing with the Arikara. Chouteau was told to find the Arikara party responsible for attacking Nathaniel Pryor's expedition and bring its members back to St. Louis as prisoners. If the Arikara did not surrender any men, Chouteau was to select three warriors who had taken part in the attack and shoot them.[9]

In May 1809, Chouteau's party left St. Louis. Lewis and Clark were confident that it would succeed. With thirteen boats and more than one hundred armed men, it could not be stopped by even the most determined and hostile Missouri River bands. It would also be the first large trading party to reach the fur-rich Yellowstone region. If the furs could be returned safely to St. Louis, they would bring the partners in the Missouri River Fur Company profit enough to sustain the company for many years.

Lewis needed such a success. He was deeply in debt for land he had purchased for speculation and for money he had advanced for the work on the expedition journals. Debt was not his only problem. His position as governor was bringing him as many conflicts as it had Frederick Bates. Although he was still a hero in Washington and Philadelphia, Lewis had already made many enemies with his policies and his appointments in St. Louis.

His most determined enemy was now Frederick Bates. By the summer of 1809, Bates and Lewis held such mistrust toward each other that they hardly ever spoke. Bates opposed Lewis's policy of closing the frontier to hunting and settlement. He also disagreed with Lewis's plan for government-sponsored trading posts. Most of all, Bates did not like the governor's quick temper or his overbearing, military manner.[10] At one St. Louis social gathering, Bates snubbed Lewis, causing a public scandal and a final bitter break between the two men.

Bates may not have known that Meriwether Lewis was suffering a deep depression, drinking heavily, and taking drugs to cope with attacks of malaria. (Carried by mosquitoes, this recurring illness causes chills, headaches, and a high fever. Lewis may have caught it during the western expedition.) The many problems of his job, his debts, and his loneliness were weighing on his mind. He had sought a wife after his return to civilization; at the age of thirty-four, he was still unmarried. Worst of all, he had done no work on his journals. Jefferson and Conrad were pestering him to start the work or to find someone else to do it for him.

Thomas Jefferson had always been Lewis's strongest ally. But now Jefferson was out of office. His administration had been replaced by that of the new president, James Madison. Frederick Bates took advantage of the change to write several complaints about Lewis during the spring and summer of 1809. The new secretary of war, William Eustis, took notice of the many drafts Lewis had signed to supply the Chouteau expedition. Eustis believed the government was liable for only seven thousand dollars, as stated in the contract with the Missouri River Fur Company. In a letter to Lewis, Eustis explained that the War Department would not honor the additional drafts. Lewis would have to pay them himself.[11]

Lewis knew this could bankrupt him. Word of Eustis's letter spread quickly. The many people who had lent money to Lewis began to demand payment. Lewis had to sell most of his property and beg for time to straighten out the problem.

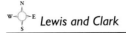

Final Voyage

Lewis prepared to travel back to Washington to meet with William Eustis and plead his case. He packed clothing, artifacts he had collected during the expedition, and his journals. He would sail as far as New Orleans, then find a ship to bring him to Washington. Clark planned to make the same journey overland, as soon as he had time.

On September 4, Lewis set off down the Mississippi with his servant, John Pernier. He now had time to think about a situation that seemed more formidable and dangerous than any he had faced before. Alcohol, illness, the letter from Eustis, Frederick Bates, the problems of the Missouri River country, and loneliness all affected him. By the time the boat reached Fort Pickering, he was delirious. The boat crew reported to Gilbert Russell, the fort's commander, that Lewis had tried to kill himself twice. Russell took Lewis off the boat and placed him under close watch.

After a few days, Lewis began to come around. He decided to go the rest of the way overland. British ships, which sometimes preyed on American shipping, and privateers in the Atlantic Ocean posed the danger of a robbery at sea, and the loss of his journals would be devastating. With Major James Neelly, an officer at Fort Pickering, Lewis and Pernier set out on the Natchez Trace, which crossed the forests and mountains of Tennessee. On October 9, two of their horses strayed. Neelly would stay behind to find them, then catch up to Lewis at the next inn.

Lewis went ahead and stopped for the night at a lonely inn called Grinder's Stand. The innkeeper was away; his wife lived in one of the inn's two cabins. After settling himself into the other cabin, Lewis spent several hours pacing his room and muttering to himself. Fearing that Lewis was a deranged man, Mrs. Grinder locked herself in her own cabin.

In the middle of the night, Mrs. Grinder heard two shots from the visitor's cabin. A short time later, Lewis crawled across to her cabin, begging for water. He had suffered gunshot wounds in the head and chest—whether by his own hand or by another's is still debated by historians. Too frightened to open the door, Mrs. Grinder moved away. Lewis crawled back to his cabin. At dawn on October 11, Pernier found Lewis slashing himself with a razor. Captain Meriwether Lewis, thirty-five years old, died a few moments later, just after sunrise.

8

WILLIAM CLARK IN ST. LOUIS

I nstead of traveling straight on to Washington after the end of the western expedition, William Clark had stopped in Virginia. Now thirty-six years old, he was determined to find a wife and settle down. He began calling on Julia (Judith) Hancock, a woman he had met in Virginia, before the expedition. On the westward leg of the expedition, he had even named Judith's River, a southern tributary of the Missouri, after her. The couple were soon planning their wedding.

In his letters to President Jefferson, Meriwether Lewis insisted that Clark share equally in the money and land to be awarded for leading the expedition. But the decision had to be made by Congress, which spent a month in early 1807 debating pay and land grants. Like Lewis, Clark was finally awarded sixteen hundred acres of land. But Congress agreed to pay him only thirty dollars a month for his service during the expedition, ten dollars a month less than Meriwether Lewis. The difference was due to Clark's lower official rank of lieutenant.

As with Lewis, the government awarded Clark a political appointment: superintendent of Indian affairs of the Louisiana Territory. Clark would also have command of the Louisiana militia and was awarded the rank of brigadier general of the militia. His principal task was to carry out Thomas Jefferson's Indian policy: removal of the eastern tribes to the Great Plains, negotiation of peace treaties with the tribes already living in the Louisiana Territory, and the construction of trading posts to control Indian trade.

With these actions, Jefferson and Clark hoped to resettle Indians out of the path of American expansion; to keep the peace with the western tribes; and to encourage the Sioux, the Oto, and the other tribes to turn from nomadic hunting to settled farming. The first important step was to return Big White to the Mandan villages. This action would win the trust of the Mandan, whom the government wanted as trading allies. Lewis and Clark spent some time making plans for Big White's voyage home. Then, in March 1807, Clark and his wife set out for St. Louis.

Working and Living with Meriwether Lewis

In St. Louis, William Clark's career closely followed that of Meriwether Lewis. In the public's view, the two men formed the inseparable halves of a team. But Clark and Lewis played different roles. As governor, Lewis had political control of Louisiana and was responsible for leading the unruly and restless populace of an early frontier territory. As commander of the Louisiana militia, Clark was responsible for defending the frontier against the British and the Spanish. He served as the leading diplomat to the Plains tribes living west of the Mississippi. He also advised Lewis on the proper actions to take to make Lewis's new trading policy a success. Clark's first important action was to organize Nathaniel Pryor's 1807 expedition to return Big White to the Mandans. The failed Pryor expedition would play an important part in the trouble faced by Lewis and Clark during the next two years.

In the summer of 1808, under Lewis's instructions, Clark led his own expedition up the Osage River to establish a trading post. The post would help the governor control trade on the river and confront the Great Osage tribe, which remained hostile to the United States. But while Lewis sought to fight and defeat hostile tribes, Clark was often able to strike a peaceful bargain with them. After building Fort Osage, Clark made his first agreement with Indians in the Louisiana Territory. The treaty set an eastern boundary line for the Great and Little Osage that the tribes were not to cross. In return for observing this line, the Osage were granted trading rights with the United States. They were also given blacksmithing and milling equipment Clark had brought west from Virginia.

Clark and Lewis remained good friends, even as the problems of the Louisiana Territory swirled around them. Clark and Lewis even shared a home with Clark's wife and niece as well as the two men's servants. Clark loaned money to Lewis to help his friend meet his debts; the two men also continued their land speculations. But the close relationship between Lewis and Clark sparked the suspicion and jealousy of Frederick Bates, Lewis's secretary. Bates watched Lewis take Clark into his confidence, while the governor did his best to keep Bates—his own secretary—out of important decisions. The bitterness Bates felt at this treatment inspired him to write damaging letters to Washington, criticizing Lewis's actions in Louisiana.

At the same time, William Clark was playing an important role in the founding of the Missouri River Fur Company. When the company was formed, he signed on as its financial officer. In this position, he handled the company's bills, debts, loans, and purchases of supplies and trade goods. He proved to be a careful record keeper and a fair-minded businessman. But the drafts Lewis signed for the company's Big White expedition, which left St. Louis in May 1809, soon got the Louisiana governor into serious trouble. The government refused to pay most of these debts. To straighten out the mess, Clark and Lewis agreed that both would go to Washington. The two men would leave separately; Lewis would take the Mississippi River downstream and then sail for Washington from New Orleans. Clark would ride east from St. Louis.

Suffering depression and a great fear for his future, Lewis set out from the docks of St. Louis on September 4, 1809. William Clark would never see him again.

Preparing the Journals

On October 18, in Nashville, James Neelly wrote a letter to break the news of Meriwether Lewis's death to Thomas Jefferson, the man who had sent Lewis west to the Pacific Ocean: "It is with extreme pain that I have to inform you of the death of His Excellency Meriwether Lewis, Governor of upper Louisiana, who died on the morning of the 11th Instant and I am sorry to say by Suicide."[1]

One week before, Neelly had buried Meriwether Lewis in a clearing a short distance from the rough, wooden cabins of Grinder's Stand. He had then collected Lewis's baggage, which still held the expedition journals, and sent it ahead to the former president. On October 28, William Clark, who was also on his way to Washington, read of Lewis's death in a Kentucky newspaper. Clark knew that Lewis had been troubled. Now he realized that these troubles had finally overcome his friend.[2]

Clark, who had named his first son Meriwether Lewis Clark, realized that the expedition journals would serve as the legacy of Lewis's short life. But Clark felt he was not qualified for the hard work of sorting out and carefully editing the journals. Nor did Jefferson have any interest in doing the work. In early 1810, Clark invited Nicholas Biddle of Philadelphia to prepare the journals for publication.[3] A brilliant scholar who had married a wealthy woman, Biddle had the time and the ability to do the job. In 1814, the firm of Bradford and Inskeep would finally publish the *History of the Expedition Under the Command of Captains Lewis and Clark.*

War on the River

When he returned to St. Louis, Clark discovered that the Missouri River Fur Company was running into financial trouble. War over land and control of

Suicide or Murder?

Historians have long argued about the death of Meriwether Lewis. Richard Dillon, one of Lewis's biographers, believed that Lewis was murdered. Dillon hinted that the Grinders, Neelly, John Pernier, Neelly's servant, or perhaps Gilbert Russell, the commander of Fort Pickering, might have been involved. He believes the motive was robbery, and notes that many of Lewis's possessions, including his rifle and horse, were stolen after his death.

Other writers believe it was suicide. Historian Stephen E. Ambrose asked, "Had William Clark entertained the slightest suspicion that his friend had been murdered, can anyone doubt that he would have gone to Tennessee immediately to find and hang the murderer? Or, if Jefferson had such suspicion, that he would have insisted the government launch an investigation?"[4]

Clark and Jefferson did not take these actions, and most historians disagree with Dillon. Still, the death of the courageous and energetic captain remains a mystery that still puzzles many historians and biographers.

the fur trade was brewing between the United States and Great Britain on the western frontier; an embargo on trade with the British had closed off an important market for the fur pelts brought in by the company's agents. The members of the firm squabbled over the prices to be charged for their goods, and the War of 1812 ended trapping expeditions up the Missouri River. William Clark and other partners had to advance the firm money in order to keep it going. Eventually, the partners agreed to cut their losses and dissolve the company.

In 1812, Congress organized the Missouri Territory, which included land in the Louisiana Purchase north of the modern northern boundary of the state of Louisiana. The Congress appointed Clark as Missouri's first territorial governor. Clark's main responsibility was to protect Missouri from British attack. His defenses were slim; late in 1813 the federal government moved an important infantry regiment east to protect the Ohio River town of Cincinnati. Clark believed that the British were allying with hostile tribes in the upper Mississippi valley to attack American settlements. He also feared an attack on St. Louis from a British outpost at Prairie du Chien, on the east bank of the Mississippi to the north. He ordered the friendly Sac and Fox Indians moved south, to keep them away from the British, and ordered four gunboats built for an expedition up the Mississippi to attack and occupy Prairie du Chien.

In the late spring of 1814, Clark personally led the expedition away from the docks of St. Louis. On June 2, when the small but well-armed fleet approached the enemy camp, Clark discovered that the British soldiers and their Indian allies had already fled. Clark occupied Prairie du Chien and raised the first American flag in what was to become Wisconsin. He then asked Major Zachary Taylor to remain with a small force and raise a fort. Clark left two of the gunboats at the site and returned to St. Louis. But just a few weeks later, on July 17, Fort Shelby was attacked and seized by tribes allied to the British. The British returned to Prairie du Chien and remained a threat to St. Louis until the war was ended by the Treaty of Ghent in December 1814. As a result of the war and the treaty, the British were held north of the Great Lakes and were no longer able to interfere in the fur trade in the Missouri Territory.

William Clark's most pressing problem was now conflict between white settlers and Indian tribes living in the trans-Mississippi region. Trusted by the American Indians, Clark was able to arrange treaty councils with the tribes and negotiate agreements that were signed at Portage des Sioux, on the Mississippi River, in the summer of 1815. By these treaties, both sides were to keep the peace and to release all prisoners. In return, the Indians were granted annuities (annual payments) of food and supplies by the government. Clark's sympathy for the tribes and his able handling of the treaty councils gave him high standing among the Indians, who often came to him to resolve their problems and disputes with the whites.

Statehood

Among white Missourians, however, Clark was losing popularity. Farmers moving into the territory wanted the United States to remove the Indians, not negotiate treaties with them. They believed that Clark was far too sympathetic to the tribes whose land they sought. In addition, Clark's ideas for developing the fur trade under government control angered Missourians who favored private enterprise, free of government interference and regulation. Clark was seen by many Missourians as part of a privileged and wealthy St. Louis elite who exercised autocratic power over the territory's economy and politics.

Reappointed as territorial governor in 1817, Clark announced himself as a candidate for the first state governor as Missouri prepared to apply for statehood in 1820. During the campaign, however, he returned to Virginia, where he attended to his wife, who was suffering a serious illness after the birth of their fifth child, John Julius Clark. On June 27, 1820, Julia Clark died. Clark then returned to Missouri, where he lost the gubernatorial election to Alexander McNair by a 3-to-1 margin.

On November 28, 1821, William Clark got married for a second time to Harriet Kennerly, with whom he had two sons before she died in 1831.

Clark remained out of favor with a large portion of the Missouri public. But his great skill in treaty negotiations, and the trust he held among Indians, won him an appointment as the first federal superintendent of Indian affairs in 1822. Clark had responsibility for a new government department, known as the Indian Bureau, which was responsible for federal policy toward American Indians.

For the rest of his life, Clark would pursue the goal of Indian resettlement and assimilation. Like Thomas Jefferson, Clark believed that the western tribes needed only to become private landowners and farmers, and to be physically separated from white society, in order to successfully make the transition from a nomadic life to a settled one. He wrote:

> Now that they are weak and harmless, and most of their lands fallen into our hands, justice and humanity require us to cherish and befriend them. To teach them to live in houses, to raise grain and stock, to plant orchards, to set up landmarks, to divide their possessions, to establish laws for their government, to get the rudiments of common learning, such as reading, writing, and ciphering.[5]

Clark believed that to achieve these goals, the Indians must move west, beyond the territorial limits, where they could live free of white interference.

Indians lived together in large villages, like the one pictured here. The powerful tide of white settlements in the West would eventually destroy this tradition.

He and other federal officials did not yet realize that the powerful tide of white settlement was just beginning its destruction of traditional Indian life on the Great Plains.

During the 1830s, when he reached his sixties, Clark again enjoyed prestige among Missourians for his leadership of the Lewis and Clark expedition and for his service as territorial governor. But the death of his friend Meriwether Lewis would always haunt him. Clark had always supported Lewis in his troubles, and the two had remained close. At first, Clark had believed the reports of Lewis's suicide.

Later, however, out of respect for the memory of his friend, he changed his mind. He denied that Lewis had taken his own life, and he could not speak of Lewis's death without great sadness.[6] William Clark remained in St. Louis for the rest of his life and died there on September 1, 1838, at the age of sixty-eight.

9

THE LEGACY OF LEWIS AND CLARK

The Lewis and Clark expedition began a rush of explorers, traders, and settlers into the Pacific Northwest. But who actually owned this territory? For many years, the question was unanswered. Any nation with a claim could explore and settle the land, and British explorers were closely following Lewis and Clark into the new frontier. In the summer of 1805, François Larocque of the North West Company, a British firm, traveled up the Yellowstone River. That winter, Simon Fraser built a British trading post on the Pacific Coast of what is now British Columbia. Fraser's post was the first such station on the Pacific Coast. It was to be the first of many such posts planned by Alexander Mackenzie and the North West Company.

Traveling south from Canada, David Thompson of the North West Company explored Idaho, Montana, and the Columbia River valley in 1807. In 1811, Thompson reached the mouth of the Columbia on another expedition. Just a few months earlier, the Pacific Fur Company, a firm established by the American fur tycoon John Jacob Astor, raised Fort Astoria along the Columbia River. This post, on the southern bank of the river, gave the United States an even stronger claim to the region and to its fur trade.

The race for the Columbia and for the Pacific Northwest continued for three decades after the building of Fort Astoria. After the Hudson's Bay Company established an outpost at Fort Vancouver, on the northern bank of the Columbia, the British and American outposts served as rival frontier capitals. But the Oregon country, as it was known, lay much too far away for British colonists, for whom sea voyages to Africa, India, and even Australia were easier than the trip to western North America. By the early 1840s, American settlers were traveling the Oregon Trail that crossed the Rocky Mountains from the Great Plains. John McLoughlin, the British commander of Fort Vancouver, became a citizen of the United States.

Fort Astoria

After Lewis and Clark blazed the Columbia River route in 1805, the race was on. Explorers of the North West Company followed with expeditions of their own down the Yellowstone and to the Columbia valley. But in the race for the northwestern fur trade, an American businessman named John Jacob Astor defeated both companies.

Several years after Lewis and Clark returned from their expedition, Astor hired North West agents to work for his own Pacific Fur Company. In 1811, Astor sent a large company west to the Columbia River. His agents settled at a point of land on the south side of Gray's Bay. There, they built Fort Astoria, the first Oregon fur post. Astor's establishment later brought rapid American settlement of the Oregon country and, eventually, American ownership of the Columbia valley.

In 1844 an American presidential candidate, James K. Polk, promised to fight, if necessary, to protect his country's claim to the Pacific Northwest.

The United States and Great Britain finally settled their differences over the region in 1846. By the Oregon Treaty, the two nations established the modern boundary of the United States and Canada at the 49th parallel. The states of Washington, Idaho, Montana, North Dakota, and Minnesota all share this imaginary line as their northern border.

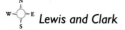

The Columbia River forms the boundary between the states of Washington and Oregon.

The Columbia River would later form the boundary between two states, Washington and Oregon.

Meanwhile, American Indians who had lived and hunted in the area for centuries were driven out by theft and by treaty. The Nez Percé, Walla Walla, and Shoshone tribes, who had helped Lewis and Clark and their men survive the western expedition, were subdued by military campaigns in the northern Rocky Mountains. They were forced to sign treaties that compelled them to live on remote or barren reservations—land forbidden to white settlement—in Washington, Idaho, and Montana. In the years following their first contact with the United States, in the form of the Lewis and Clark expedition, many members of the northwestern tribes died of smallpox, measles, and influenza brought by the whites.

Along the route traveled by Lewis and Clark now stand signs and memorials to the expedition of 1804–1806. Many of the expedition's campsites have been discovered, and in some places, the trails used by the explorers can still be followed.[1] Because the journals took so long to be published, many of the names the two captains gave to the rivers and landmarks along their way were replaced by later ones. But their legacy continues, and with the passing of almost two hundred years since their return to St. Louis, their accomplishments have grown in interest and importance.

William Clark is remembered as one of the most important figures of early frontier history, and a founding father of the territory and state of Missouri. As a trusted negotiator in Indian affairs, his words and deeds stand in contrast to later treaty making in the West, when the drive for land grew more important than the honoring of promises and treaties by the United States government.

Meriwether Lewis remains one of the most fascinating and tragic figures in United States

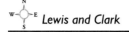

Lewis and Clark blazed trails through the Rocky Mountains that were followed by thousands of pioneers.

history. He ranks high both as a naturalist and as an explorer. Besides establishing the first American claim to the Pacific Northwest, he also discovered new specimens of flora and fauna. With Clark, he surmounted near-impossible odds in the wilderness and blazed trails through the Rocky Mountains that would later be followed by thousands of pioneers. Yet he ended his own life at a young age, overwhelmed by the mundane, everyday problems of money, loneliness, and politics.

Together, Meriwether Lewis and William Clark became the first to show the people of the United States the true extent and enormous potential of the continent they were about to explore, seize, and make their own.

CHRONOLOGY

1770—William Clark born on August 1, in Albemarle County, Virginia.

1774—Meriwether Lewis born on August 18, in Albemarle County.

1776—Declaration of Independence signed.

1783—Treaty of Paris ends the Revolutionary War; Great Britain cedes lands east of the Mississippi River and south of the Great Lakes to the United States.

1784—William Clark moves with his family to Kentucky.

1789—William Clark enlists in the United States Army; Alexander Mackenzie fails to discover a Northwest Passage to the Pacific Ocean.

1792—Robert Gray, an American ship captain, discovers and names the Columbia River.

1793—Mackenzie reaches the Pacific, becoming the first white man to cross the northern Rocky Mountains.

1794—Meriwether Lewis volunteers for the Virginia militia during the Whiskey Rebellion.

1795—Lewis joins the United States Army; Later in the year, he is transferred to William Clark's Chosen Rifle Company.

1796—Clark retires from the army.

1800—By the Treaty of San Ildefonso, France gains the Louisiana Territory from Spain.

1801—Thomas Jefferson is inaugurated as president of the United States; He invites Meriwether Lewis to serve as his personal secretary.

1802—Jefferson and Lewis begin planning a Missouri River expedition.

1803—France sells Louisiana to the United States for $15 million; Lewis sets out from Pittsburgh; Clark joins him at the Falls of the Ohio.

1804—The Lewis and Clark expedition sets out from St. Louis; They reach the Mandan villages of the upper Missouri River and make a winter camp.

1805—Lewis and Clark cross the Continental Divide and follow the Columbia River to its mouth on the Pacific Ocean; They winter at Fort Clatsop.

1806—Lewis and Clark separate their parties to recross the Divide; They join at the mouth of the Yellowstone River and reach St. Louis in September.

1807—Jefferson appoints Lewis governor of Louisiana; Clark serves as superintendent for Indian affairs and brigadier general of the Louisiana militia.

1808—Lewis reaches St. Louis one year after his appointment; Clark marries Julia Hancock; St. Louis Missouri River Fur Company formed.

1809—The government protests drafts signed by Lewis in St. Louis; Facing financial ruin, Lewis sets out for Washington; On October 11, he commits suicide at Grinder's Stand, Tennessee.

1812—Clark appointed territorial governor of Missouri.

1814—The journals of Lewis and Clark are published, after two years of editing by Nicholas Biddle.

1815—William Clark negotiates the Portage des Sioux treaties with several tribes of the Missouri River region.

1817—Clark is reappointed as governor of the Missouri Territory.

1820—Clark runs for governor of Missouri but is defeated.

1822—Clark is appointed federal superintendent of Indian affairs.

1830—Clark helps to write the Treaty of Prairie du Chien.

1838—Clark dies in St. Louis.

1846—By the Oregon Treaty, Great Britain and the United States agree on the boundary between the Oregon Territory and Canada.

CHAPTER NOTES

Chapter 1. At Marias River

1. Bernard DeVoto, ed., *The Journals of Lewis and Clark* (Boston: Houghton Mifflin Company, 1953), p. 125.

2. David Lavender, *The Way to the Western Sea: Lewis and Clark Across the Continent* (New York: Harper & Row, 1988), pp. 205–206; DeVoto, p. 127.

3. DeVoto, p. 128.

4. Ibid., p. 134.

Chapter 2. The Lewises of Locust Hill

1. Stephen E. Ambrose, *Undaunted Courage: Meriwether Lewis, Thomas Jefferson, and the Opening of the American West* (New York: Simon & Schuster, 1996), pp. 19–24; Richard Dillon, *Meriwether Lewis: A Biography* (New York: Coward-McCann, Inc., 1965), pp. 6–9.

2. Ambrose, p. 37.

3. Ibid., p. 39; Dillon, pp. 18–19.

4. Ambrose, pp. 39–43.

5. Dillon, p. 21.

6. Donald Jackson, *Letters of the Lewis and Clark Expedition* (Urbana, Ill.: University of Illinois Press, 1962), pp. 2–3.

7. Ibid., p. 3.

8. Ibid.

Chapter 3. The Clarks of Caroline County

1. Charles Van Doren and Robert McHenry, eds., *Webster's Guide to American History* (Springfield, Mass.: G & C Merriam Co., 1971), pp. 1327–1328; James MacGregor Burns, *The Vineyard of Liberty* (New York: Alfred A. Knopf, 1982), pp. 196–197.

2. Jerome O. Steffan, *William Clark: Jeffersonian Man on the Frontier* (Norman, Okla.: University of Oklahoma Press, 1977), p. 24.

Chapter 4. Racing for the Northwest Passage

1. Bernard DeVoto, ed., *The Journals of Lewis and Clark* (Boston: Houghton Mifflin Company, 1953), p. xxv; Stephen E. Ambrose, *Undaunted Courage: Meriwether Lewis, Thomas Jefferson, and the Opening of the American West* (New York: Simon & Schuster, 1996), p. 54.

2. David Lavender, *The Way to the Western Sea: Lewis and Clark Across the Continent* (New York: Harper & Row, 1988), p. 31.

3. Richard Dillon, *Meriwether Lewis: A Biography* (New York: Coward-McCann, Inc., 1965), pp. 6–11.

4. Ibid., p. 3.

5. Donald Jackson, *Letters of the Lewis and Clark Expedition* (Urbana, Ill.: University of Illinois Press, 1962), pp. 669–672.

6. DeVoto, p. xx.

7. Ibid., pp. xxii, xxiii.

8. Jackson, pp. 589–590.

9. Ambrose, p. 79.

10. Ibid., p. 77.

11. Ambrose, p. 101; DeVoto, p. xxiii.

12. Floyd Shoemaker, "The Louisiana Purchase, 1803," *Missouri Historical Review*, vol. 48, October 1953, p. 9; Ambrose, p. 101.

13. Ambrose, p. 88; Jackson, pp. 93–99.

14. Jackson, pp. 57–60.

15. Ibid., pp. 110–111.

Chapter 5. Down the Ohio, Up the Missouri

1. Donald Jackson, *Letters of the Lewis and Clark Expedition* (Urbana, Ill.: University of Illinois Press, 1962), pp. 61–66.

2. Stephen E. Ambrose, *Undaunted Courage: Meriwether Lewis, Thomas Jefferson, and the Opening of the American West* (New York: Simon & Schuster, 1996), p. 95; Richard Dillon, *Meriwether Lewis: A Biography* (New York: Coward-McCann, Inc., 1965), p. 54.

3. Dillon, p. 56.

4. Jackson, p. 117.

5. Ambrose, pp. 115–116.

6. Jackson, p. 179.

7. Bernard DeVoto, ed., *The Journals of Lewis and Clark* (Boston: Houghton Mifflin Company, 1953), pp. 489–491.

8. Ambrose, p. 89.

9. Jackson, pp. 203–208.

10. DeVoto, p. 74.

Chapter 6. End of the Expedition

1. Donald Jackson, *Letters of the Lewis and Clark Expedition* (Urbana, Ill.: University of Illinois Press, 1962), pp. 231–236.

2. Bernard DeVoto, ed., *The Journals of Lewis and Clark* (Boston: Houghton Mifflin Company, 1953), p. 103.

3. Ibid., p. 105.

4. Ibid., p. 106.

5. Ibid., p. 118.

6. Albert Salisbury and Jane Salisbury, *Lewis & Clark: The Journey West* (New York: Promontory Press, 1950), pp. 147–149.

7. David Lavender, *The Way to the Western Sea: Lewis and Clark Across the Continent* (New York: Harper & Row, 1988), pp. 397–400.

8. Ibid., pp. 474–475.

9. Jackson, pp. 330–335.

10. Ibid., pp. 319–324.

11. DeVoto, p. 478.

Chapter 7. Meriwether Lewis After the Expedition

1. Stephen E. Ambrose, *Undaunted Courage: Meriwether Lewis, Thomas Jefferson, and the Opening of the American West* (New York: Simon & Schuster, 1996), p. 429.

2. Ibid., p. 446.

3. Richard Dillon, *Meriwether Lewis: A Biography* (New York: Coward-McCann, Inc., 1965), p. 279.

4. Donald Jackson, *Letters of the Lewis and Clark Expedition* (Urbana, Ill.: University of Illinois Press, 1962), p. 406; Dillon, p. 283.

5. John Logan Allen, *Passage Through the Garden* (Urbana, Ill.: University of Illinois Press, 1975), p. 373; Jackson, pp. 394–397.

6. Jackson, pp. 432–437.

7. Ambrose, pp. 440–444.

8. Jackson, pp. 446–450.

9. Ibid., pp. 451–456.

10. Ambrose, pp. 465–466; Dillon, pp. 314–315; 327–328.

11. Jackson, pp. 456–457.

Chapter 8. William Clark in St. Louis

1. Donald Jackson, *Letters of the Lewis and Clark Expedition* (Urbana, Ill.: University of Illinois Press, 1962), pp. 467–468.

2. Stephen E. Ambrose, *Undaunted Courage: Meriwether Lewis, Thomas Jefferson, and the Opening of the American West* (New York: Simon & Schuster, 1996), p. 476.

3. Jackson, p. 494.

4. Ambrose, pp. 467–468.

5. Jerome O. Steffan, *William Clark: Jeffersonian Man on the Frontier* (Norman, Okla.: University of Oklahoma Press, 1977), p. 133.

6. John Bakeless, ed., *The Journals of Lewis and Clark* (New York: Mentor, 1964), p. ix; Richard Dillon, *Meriwether Lewis: A Biography* (New York: Coward-McCann, Inc., 1965), p. 338.

Chapter 9. The Legacy of Lewis and Clark

1. Albert Salisbury and Jane Salisbury, *Lewis & Clark: The Journey West* (New York: Promontory Press, 1950), p. 10.

GLOSSARY

botany—The study of plants.

chronometer—A complex and accurate timepiece used to help determine longitude.

Continental Divide—An imaginary line dividing east-flowing from west-flowing rivers in the Rocky Mountains.

draft—A document that promises to pay a certain sum of money in the future.

dugout—A boat made from a hollowed-out tree trunk.

embargo—A ban on the trade of certain goods or with a certain nation.

estuary—A widening of a river as it approaches the sea.

forage—An area of grass and plants where horses can graze.

inauguration—A ceremony that begins the term of an elected official.

keelboat—A shallow riverboat that can transport passengers and goods.

malaria—A serious illness transmitted by mosquitoes, bringing on fever and fatigue.

militia—A small, temporary, or volunteer military force.

Northwest Passage—An imaginary water route across North America.

pirogue—A small, flat-bottomed boat used for river transport.

portage—To carry boats from one waterway to another across dry land.

sextant—An instrument used to measure the angle of the sun, moon, or stars above the horizon.

tributary—A smaller river that feeds the main branch of a larger waterway.

vermilion—A reddish pigment found in rocks or soil, used as paint by American Indians.

watershed—The area drained by a river and all of its tributaries.

FURTHER READING

Books

Ambrose, Stephen E. *Undaunted Courage: Meriwether Lewis, Thomas Jefferson, and the Opening of the American West*. New York: Simon & Schuster, 1996.

Cavan, Seamus. *Lewis and Clark and the Route to the Pacific*. New York: Chelsea House Publishers, 1991.

Fitz-Gerald, Christine A. *The World's Great Explorers: Meriwether Lewis and William Clark*. Chicago, Ill.: Children's Press, Inc., 1991.

Lavender, David. *The Way to the Western Sea: Lewis and Clark Across the Continent*. New York: Harper & Row, 1988.

McGrath, Patrick. *The Lewis and Clark Expedition*. Morristown, N.J.: Silver Burdett Publishers, 1985.

Old, Wendie C. *Thomas Jefferson*. Springfield, N.J.: Enslow Publishers, Inc., 1997.

Salisbury, Albert, and Jane Salisbury. *Lewis & Clark: The Journey West*. New York: Promontory Press, 1993.

Internet Sites

Great Outdoor Recreation Pages. *Lewis and Clark Trail*. n.d. <http://www.gorp.com/gorp/resource/US_TRAIL/LEWIS&CL.HTM> (April 22, 1998).

Lewis and Clark Trail Heritage Foundation. n.d. <http://www.lewisandclark.org/> (April 22, 1998).

INDEX